AROMA

AROMA

Mandy Aftel and Daniel Patterson

ARTISAN

NEW YORK

Published by Artisan

A Division of Workman Publishing, Inc.

708 Broadway, New York, New York 10003-9555

www.artisanbooks.com

Library of Congress Cataloging-in-Publication Data

Patterson, Daniel, 1968-

Aroma / by Daniel Patterson and Mandy Aftel.

    p. cm.

  Includes index.

  ISBN 1-57965-264-6

1. Cookery. 2. Essences and essential oils. 3. Odors. I. Aftel,
Mandy. II. Title.

TX714.P382 2004

  641.5—dc22   2003063915

Printed in Singapore

10 9 8 7 6 5 4 3 2 1

Book design by Vivian Ghazarian

OPPOSITE, FROM LEFT: cocoa, coffee beans, cognac,
chocolate, truffle, porcini. FOLLOWING PAGE, CLOCKWISE FROM
TOP: lime, green tea powder, mint leaves, green and red shiso
(perilla), verbena sprig.

For Chloe —M.A.

For Alexandra —D.P.

Contents

FROM LEFT TO RIGHT: jojoba oil, saffron absolute, saffron sprigs, epsom salts.

Preface

We have spent our professional careers working with aroma, Mandy as a natural perfumer and Daniel as a chef. Mandy is an avid home cook who has always seen the connection between cooking and perfumery. Good cooking and good fragrance making each start with high-quality natural ingredients that are transformed through technique to create a result that is balanced, harmonious, and magically better than the sum of its parts. Mandy had hoped to write a book exploring the relationship between flavor and aroma and, after having dinner at Daniel's restaurant, she knew that he would be the perfect collaborator because of the emphasis given to aroma in every dish.

The first time we met to talk about the book, Daniel was captivated by smelling the natural essences that Mandy had brought. As he smelled vial after vial of concentrated aroma of rose, ginger, and black pepper, each essence revealed facets of the ingredient that he never knew were there, and it was as if he were smelling those scents for the first time. The experience was revelatory. He started cooking with the essences and discovered that, used properly, they could transform dishes, making rote combinations memorable and good dishes great.

As we started to write the book, we began to realize that we were exploring an area that had mostly been ignored. While many cookbooks include some information or instruction about the use of aromatics in cooking, none concentrates on this aspect. Slowly we were drawn deeper into the interconnectedness of aroma and flavor, learning that smell is, in fact, the primary sense when eating, with taste following after, and that the immediacy of aroma and its connection to emotion and memory create the most unforgettable experiences. We talk briefly about this relationship on page 11.

In *Aroma,* we cook with fragrance and we also make perfumed items such as bath salts and fragrant mists. Fragrance making is really quite simple—it's like cooking. In "The Cooks' Pantry" and "The Perfumer's Pantry," we talk about the ingredients and equipment you will need for both, and explain the terms and techniques. You will be able to find most of what you need in grocery and cookware stores, but we provide Sources (page 201) for anything you may have trouble locating. You definitely do not need to restock your pantry in order to use the book, but when you see the results of the recipes, you may be tempted to expand it. Mandy thinks the Saffron, Ginger, and Blood Orange Bath Salts recipe (page 192) is so wonderful that it will instantly convert you to a dedicated home fragrance maker. Daniel could not believe how new and exciting he found litsea cubeba (a citruslike essential oil from China) when he first tried it, and he uses it in recipes such as Steamed Artichokes with Litsea Cubeba Mayonnaise (page 75) and Pineapple–Litsea Cubeba Granita (page 98).

The recipes are based on revealing the aromatic qualities of single ingredients, such as rosemary (page 68) or chocolate (187). These single ingredients are grouped together in the flavor categories such as Refreshing, Earthy, or Luxurious. We describe the aromatic and flavor qualities of each ingredient and what to look for when buying it. We then offer a fragrance recipe based on that ingredient, and follow it with three food recipes. Mandy wrote all of the fragrance recipes and Daniel wrote the food recipes, which allowed us to give our thoughts and feelings about how each ingredient is used and what its effect is. As you will see, there are similarities in our approaches.

There are different ways to enter the book. You can check out "Recipes for Fragrances" (page 13) and "Recipes to Cook" (page 14), where recipes are grouped under headings such as Liquid or Solid Perfumes or Bath Salts or Appetizers or Desserts. Or you can look for an ingredient that appeals to you and choose a recipe created around the ingredient. Or you can let your mood, the weather, or the season direct you toward sections such as Earthy (page 119) in the winter months, or Floral (page 91) in the summer. If you stumble on an unfamiliar term or technique, refer back to "The Perfumer's Pantry" (page 19) and "The Cook's Pantry" (page 27), where all is explained. However you find your way in, we encourage you to explore, and hope you will find new pleasure in the aromatic dimension of food, fragrance, and life.

Regarding Aroma, Emotion, and Memory

We have all had memories like the narrator of Marcel Proust's *In Search of Lost Time,* who is brought back to his childhood by the taste of crumbs of madeleine mixed with tea. For us, cinnamon evokes apple pies, holidays, warmth of family, and friends. The smell of rose recalls loves past and present; jasmine, the intoxication of spring. The process by which smell becomes fused with place or experience is actually involuntary. Smell is the only sense that connects directly to brain's limbic system—the center of taste, emotion, and memory. This direct link gives scent its emotional power, and it is why we form such strong attachments to things that smell or taste good.

In the kitchen where a stew simmers, in the living room where the dog curls up on the leather couch, on our skin where the perfume we wear mingles with body chemistry to create a scent as unique as a fingerprint, aroma imprints and vivifies emotional memory. While taste is just a handful of sensations—sweet, sour, salty, bitter, umami—aroma has an almost unlimited palette. Sniffing food as it cooks, or when it is on the plate, gives us aroma in its purest and simplest form. Savoring it in our mouth, we experience the aroma simultaneously with the taste, in a complex intermingling of sensations we call flavor. Aroma both precedes and is bound with the way we taste food. Thinking about the emotional associations attached to the dishes and fragrances you make from this book will deepen your understanding and enjoyment.

RECIPES FOR FRAGRANCES

{ RECIPES TO COOK }

The Safe Use of Natural Essences

Essential oils contain the most intense concentration of the plant they are extracted from, and so should be used carefully. All of the essential oils and other essences in this book that are used for cooking are not only FDA approved, but have relatively low toxicity. Used appropriately, all of them are completely safe. However, it is important to follow a few guidelines:

• Use only the amounts specified in the recipes, usually a few drops, or at most a fraction of a teaspoon.

• Use only pure and natural essences, not synthetic, in the making of food and fragrance.

• Do not drink essences directly from the bottles.

• Always store the essences in a locked cabinet or drawer where small children cannot get hold of them.

• If you are allergic to an ingredient, do not ingest an essence derived from that ingredient. If you have tried an ingredient before and are not sure if you are allergic to it, do not use the essence derived from that ingredient until a doctor or other expert has determined that you are not allergic to that ingredient.

• Do not use or ingest essences if you are pregnant.

Some natural essences, when applied directly to the skin, have been known to cause allergic reactions. Even though natural essences in perfumery are diluted in alcohol or other carriers, if you are prone to allergies or have sensitive skin, it may be advisable to try a patch test to see if a particular oil is problematic for you. Apply one drop of the oil in question to the inside of your forearm and cover it with an adhesive strip. After a few hours, check for redness or irritation. Do not use any essence to which you have a reaction. The International Fragrance Association (IFRA) has compiled a list of recommended guidelines for commercial perfumers, which is updated periodically. You can find it on the Web at www.ifraorg.org/guidelines.asp.

The Perfumer's Pantry

Natural plant essences—essential oils, hydrosols, concretes, absolutes, resins, and balsams—are the building blocks of complex and evocative scents. Sometimes the fragrance resides in the rind of the fruit, as with blood orange and pink grapefruit; sometimes in the roots, as with ginger; sometimes in the woody stem, as with cedarwood or sandalwood, or in the bark, as with cinnamon; sometimes in the leaves, as with mint, basil, and thyme; sometimes in the seeds, as with cardamom and cumin; and sometimes in the flower, as with rose and jasmine. Perfume essences exist in many forms and on many levels of intensity. In developing one's palette of natural essences, it is important to understand the variations on a theme—the subtle difference between a jasmine absolute and a jasmine concrete, for example. Even slightly different forms of the same odor have different values when working with fragrance, not only in terms of technical issues like staying power, but for their own inherent sensual qualities and associations.

Use only pure and natural essences for both fragrance making and cooking. Never use synthetic oils, sometimes referred to as fragrance oils. You can order with confidence from the suppliers named in the Sources (page 201) or look for them at reputable health food stores. As in cooking, try to use organic or "wild"-crafted essential oils whenever possible.

All of the essences discussed below are used in the fragrance recipes, but only essential oils and absolutes are used in the food recipes. The food recipes also incorporate or are based upon the fresh aromatic ingredients where appropriate.

Essential oils

Essential oils are the largest category of fragrance materials, and the most widely available, due to the tremendous popularity of aromatherapy. Most of the oils come from distillation, except for the oils extracted from citrus fruits, which are rendered by simple pressing. Essential oils are not the same as vegetable oils, which are

SALTS, CLOCKWISE FROM TOP: Sweet Orange, Ylang-Ylang, and Geranium Bath Salts (page 55); epsom salts; Saffron, Ginger, and Blood Orange Bath Salts (page 192); Mint, Basil, and Coriander Bath Salts (page 39). OILS, CLOCKWISE FROM CENTER: Ginger and Juniper Body Oil (page 159), bergamot essential oil, nutmeg essential oil, saffron absolute, ylang-ylang essential oil, cocoa perfume.

pressed from seeds, nuts, olive flesh, and the bran of grain. Unlike vegetable oils, essential oils are not greasy and are soluble in alcohol.

Steam distillation with water is the most widely used method for obtaining essential oils. Small pieces of oil-bearing plant material are placed in a container or a still. Steam is passed through the still, causing the oil to vaporize. The mixture of steam and oil vapor then passes through a condenser, returning to a liquid phase where the oil and water separate. The oil rendered is the essential oil, and the water left over is the hydrosol.

Hydrosols
Hydrosols, a by-product of the distillation of flowers, roots, barks, branches, needles, and leaves of plants, are what remain after the essential oil is separated from the water used in distillation. Hydrosols contain only a tiny amount of the oil, but they have plant-based properties and nutrients, which make them very different from regular water to which a few drops of essential oil has been added. Hydrosols are lighter and evaporate faster than essential oils and offer a different, more subtle olfactory experience.

Concretes and absolutes
The oils of flowers with fragrance too fragile to withstand the heat of distillation are extracted by solvents. Because the flowers give off a great deal of waxy material, the process yields a so-called concrete, which is semisolid. Concretes have great staying power, and there is a softness to their aroma that makes them perfect for use in solid perfume. (They are not completely soluble in alcohol, so if they are infused into a liquid perfume, the insoluble dregs need to be strained after the ageing process.)

By removing waxes and other solids, a concrete can be rendered into an absolute, a highly concentrated liquid essence that is completely alcohol-soluble. Much longer lasting than essential oils, absolutes have an intensity and fineness to their aroma that is unequaled. They are generally the most expensive essences.

Resins and balsams
Resins are the viscous, solid, or semisolid gums derived from trees, particularly pine and other evergreens. These thick substances have tremendous staying power.

Balsams also come from trees, but usually from incisions made in the bark. Balsams often have a cinnamon or vanilla scent. Like the resins, they help to "fix" a perfume and make it last.

Liquid perfume

Liquid perfume is the most intense and expensive form of fragrance, with the largest concentration of essential oils, absolutes, and concretes, approximately 30 percent of the finished perfume. Liquid perfume is traditionally kept in beautiful small bottles (one-quarter to one ounce) fitted with ground glass stoppers. Natural perfume blossoms on the skin and should not be simply smelled from the bottle.

Blending essences to make perfume requires a carrier or medium. By far the most common carrier for liquid perfumes is 190-proof ethyl alcohol, which mixes completely with essential oils and absolutes and will dilute the thickest of resins, balsams, and concretes. It also helps to lift and diffuse the essences, allowing them to blossom as aromas.

Isopropyl (or rubbing) alcohol is strong smelling and unsuitable for perfume making. You may be able to find good-quality ethyl alcohol at some drugstores (ask in the pharmacy) or at local or mail order chemical supply houses (see Sources, 201). Alcohol is very flammable and should be stored well away from sunlight and heaters.

Cologne

Cologne has a lower concentration of fragrant ingredients, about 4 percent. Historically, 190-proof grape alcohol is the carrier of choice for cologne. With its fruity, clean, fresh smell, it blends beautifully with citruses, herbs, and floral essences. When using cologne, try spraying it on your hair, which acts as a natural fixative.

Solid perfume

Very convenient, solid perfume can be carried almost anywhere without spilling or leaking. It also tends to be simpler than a liquid perfume; one or two essences will make a beautiful solid perfume.

The base of solid perfume is beeswax and jojoba oil (pronounced ho-HO-ba). Jojoba oil, from the seeds of a desert shrub, is a lovely golden color, with no fragrance of its own. An excellent moisturizer, jojoba is much less prone to rancidity and oxidation than other oils. Natural yellow beeswax lends a sweet fragrance and warm amber color to solid perfumes. The process of grating, melting, and smelling the wax's delicate honeyed scent contributes to the meditative aspects of making solid perfume. Bleached beeswax is also available but not recommended because its texture is thin, the bleaching gives the wax a chemical smell, and the resulting perfume is pasty in texture and appearance.

A solid perfume should be the texture of a creamy lipstick, adhering easily to your finger. Ideal solid perfume texture depends upon the correct proportion of beeswax to jojoba oil. Too much wax makes the perfume hard and unyielding; too little wax makes the perfume runny. Apply solid perfume by running the ball of your finger back and forth across the surface of the perfume; do not use your fingertip to scoop it out, as using the tip leaves an unsightly marred surface.

A container for solid perfume should be round, oval, or square, but not triangular because it is hard to get the perfume out of the corners. Shallow containers are also preferable, because it is difficult to get the perfume out of a deeper basin. Small compacts and pillboxes are perfect, and they are easy to find at flea markets or online. A secure latch or lid is important.

Bath salts

Bath salts are simple to make and are wonderful gifts. Fine Dead Sea salts (see Sources, page 201) will dissolve thoroughly in a warm tub, but you can also use other sea salts or epsom salts from a drugstore. Using natural bath salts is a slightly different process from using those created with synthetic essences. Chemicals make synthetic essences long lasting. Natural essences volatize immediately when exposed to hot water. Therefore, do not add the salts while the water is running. Add them only after the tub is full and you are in it. Close the bathroom door to trap the scent. To revitalize the scent, agitate the water a bit.

USEFUL TOOLS

Alcohol

Use 190-proof undenatured alcohol to dissolve resins and thick oils when cleaning droppers. You can also use rubbing alcohol for this purpose, although it is not as effective.

Beakers

Beakers to use for blending are available from chemical supply houses. Ones that are small, wide, and calibrated every five milliliters are most useful.

Filters

A simple plastic coffee filter and unbleached filter paper can be used for straining perfumes. When straining more than one perfume, throw away the used filter paper and rinse the filter in clean alcohol to eliminate the previous scent.

Glass droppers

Use glass droppers, not plastic pipettes, for measuring essences and other ingredients. They can be bought in a drugstore or by the dozen at chemical supply houses (see Sources, page 201).

Grater

You will need a grater to grate beeswax. A simple box grater used for cheese is fine. Use the medium-size holes and grate one cup at a time. Store the grated beeswax in a resealable plastic bag.

Hot plate

You can use a gas or electric burner for melting wax. If you become more serious about making solid perfume, get a small hot plate from a laboratory supply company. Do not use alcohol near open flames because it is extremely flammable.

Measuring spoons

Use measuring spoons for larger quantities of ingredients. Try to find a set that has a one-eighth-teaspoon measure.

Nonmetal pan for melting wax

Use a small nonmetal pan for melting wax. Ceramic or glass is best. Chemical supply houses sell tiny heatproof ceramic pans that are perfect for small batches of solid perfume. Small ramekins or soufflé dishes from your kitchen are also suitable.

Scent strips

Fragrance scent strips are an essential tool for exploring the world of fragrance. Scent strips resemble five-inch-long paddles—made of stiff but absorbent unscented paper—and taper to about a quarter of an inch at one end. Write the name of the material you are sampling on the thicker end and dip a half inch of the other end into the essence, then smell it. Scent strips can be purchased (see Sources, page 201) or you can simply cut thick watercolor paper into narrow strips.

Stirring sticks

Use bamboo skewers or wooden chopsticks for stirring perfume blends. Glass cocktail stirrers, if you come across them in a thrift shop, are wonderful for this use. Bamboo skewers need to be cut into manageable lengths so that they are not too much taller than the beaker you are using. If they are too tall, the beaker will likely tip over while you are working. Small salt spoons also work for stirring blends.

Fragrance making is simple, quick, and rewarding. Measure out essences by the drop and stir them into bath salts, oils, or alcohol. Here are some fragrance-making terms, concepts, and techniques you will encounter in this book.

Top, middle, and base notes

Essences are classified according to their volatility, or how long they remain perceptibly fragrant before the scent fades. Top (or head) notes are the most fleeting, less so are middle (or heart) notes, and base notes last longest. The most important quality to consider when creating a blend is volatility.

Base notes, intense and profound, are often thick and syrupy. Most are derived from bark (sandalwood), roots (angelica), resins (labdanum), lichens (oakmoss), saps (benzoin, Peru balsam), and grasses (patchouli, vetiver).

Middle notes give body to blends, imparting warmth and fullness. They include most flowers: geranium, rose, jasmine, orange flower, tuberose, and ylang-ylang.

Top notes are bright and fleeting, and often familiar from cooking: herbs and spices such as coriander, spearmint, black pepper, cardamom, juniper, and tarragon, and citruses such as lime, bitter orange, blood orange, tangerine, and pink grapefruit. Most essential oils are top notes.

You can test whether an essence is a top, middle, or base note by dipping a scent strip in the essence and smelling the strip over the course of the next several hours. Top notes lose their scent rather quickly (around two hours), middle notes take more time (around twelve hours), and strong base notes do not fully evolve for many hours, and may last for several days or longer. When you become practiced enough, you will be able to determine for yourself whether a given essence is a top, middle, or base note. Group your essences together by top, middle, and base notes, so you may "see" the blending possibilities more clearly as you build a fragrance.

Accessory notes

Essences with exceptionally high odor strength—for example, where one drop of an essence is as powerful as ten drops of another—are known as accessory notes. Examples include black pepper, patchouli, petitgrain, litsea cubeba, clove, rosemary, and cinnamon. Accessory notes cannot be used in large amounts in a formula without disaster. However, their trace presence in a formula can transform a blend, giving it a unique cachet that verges on the alchemical.

Measuring essences

Try to buy essences with dropper caps or shaker tops. These are plastic inserts that fit in the opening of a bottle and allow you to invert the bottle and measure drop by drop. You can also use glass eye droppers (and must, for thick essences such as cèpes absolute). Here is the technique:

Obtain a shot glass or similar-size glass container, an eyedropper, ethyl or rubbing alcohol, and paper towels. Fill the shot glass halfway with the alcohol, put the dropper in the glass, and squeeze the top of the dropper to draw the alcohol into the chamber. Then empty the dropper and wipe it on a clean paper towel to remove any traces of alcohol. Insert the dropper into the essence you want to use and transfer the desired number drops into your blend. Return any unused essence to the bottle it came from. Pump the empty used dropper in the shot glass and leave it filled and soaking in the alcohol. If the alcohol looks cloudy or dirty, discard it and refill the shot glass with fresh alcohol, then reinsert the dropper and pump it full of alcohol and leave it to soak.

Setting Up Your Work Environment

Always start with a clean and organized workspace. Fold a paper towel in half. On your right, place the shot glass filled with either rubbing or ethyl alcohol and droppers. On your left, place the beaker or bowl or other receptacle and measure into it the carrier, such as jojoba oil or alcohol. Following the preceding instructions for measuring essences, measure drops of essence into your fragrance carrier. Always add the base notes first, followed by the middle notes and finally the top notes. If you add the base notes last, you will not be able to smell the top notes clearly and understand their effect on the blend. Note the aromatic changes after each addition by putting a drop on your hand and smelling it on your skin. Have all your materials available, especially when you are "cooking" a solid perfume, and do not allow any distractions or interruptions or you may overheat the blend.

Olfactory fatigue

Olfactory fatigue can set in after you smell too many essences in succession. When essences begin to smell weak, it is time to refresh the olfactory palate. The easiest way to do this is to inhale three times deeply through a piece of wool. A scarf or shawl works well for this purpose.

Storage

Natural essences are easily damaged by exposure to light and air and by radical changes in temperature. They should be stored in small glass (not plastic) bottles, with the tops tightly sealed. Always label both the bottle and the cap, because, when working with several essences, it is easy to put the wrong top on an open bottle.

The more often you open a bottle containing a natural essence, the greater the chance of oxidation, particularly with the citrus essential oils. Try not to open bottles any more often than necessary. If you buy your essential oils in large quantities, you should immediately transfer a small amount to a small bottle and keep the rest undisturbed. If the first whiff upon opening smells stale or rancid, or you notice that the oil has become thicker or hazy, the essence may have deteriorated.

Most natural essences will keep for many years. In fact, jasmine, orris, patchouli, rose, sandalwood, frankincense, and rosewood age beautifully. Citrus essential oils lose their freshness quickly. Purchase them in small quantities and store them in the refrigerator. Replace them after six months, or sooner if they begin to smell rancid or flat. Hydrosols should also be stored in the refrigerator, and replaced after four months.

Measurements

Most beakers are metric-calibrated. The metric is translated below so you can use measuring spoons instead.

0.60 milliliters = $1/8$ teaspoon
1.25 milliliters = $1/4$ teaspoon
2.50 milliliters = $1/2$ teaspoon
3.75 milliliters = $3/4$ teaspoon
5.00 milliliters = 1 teaspoon
15.00 milliliters = 1 tablespoon

The Cook's Pantry

COOKING WITH ESSENTIAL OILS

Having essential oils in your pantry is like having an herb garden in constant full bloom, except the access is easier. Whereas dried herbs tend to have a musty smell and taste nothing like their fresh counterparts, essential oils perfectly capture the qualities of the living plant, in both aroma and flavor. With the exception of the citrus oils and the hydrosols, which need to be stored in the refrigerator, essences can be kept in a cabinet, ready to use. Always buy pure and natural essences (see Sources, page 201). Never use synthetic essences, sometimes referred to as fragrance oils.

When you order the oils, ask for a shaker top. Much like the piece of plastic on the top of a bottle of hot sauce, it allows you to shake out a drop at a time without using an eyedropper. This makes adding a drop or two of essential oil to a dish as easy as unscrewing the top of the bottle. The only exception is the more viscous absolutes, such as cèpe.

Because of their strength, essential oils should be used sparingly, a drop at a time, and always diluted. As you work with them you will learn which ones are the strongest, but generally their intensity corresponds to the natural ingredients from which they are derived. For example, cinnamon and ginger are stronger than orange and mint. Through the recipes you will get an idea of how much to use, and with practice you will grow as familiar with black pepper essential oil as you are with freshly ground pepper. Always start with a drop, then taste to see how much more to add; you can always add more, but once a dish is overseasoned there is no way to adjust it.

Essential oils should always be diluted before they are used in cooking. There are a few ways to do this. One way of the best ways to dilute essential oils is in fat, as fat fixes flavor. Create a flavor-infused oil by adding a few drops of essential oil to pure olive oil or peanut oil, and then use that oil to dress a salad, toss with pasta, drizzle over soups or stews, marinate fish or meat, or cook vegetables. You can also add a drop or two to a sauce, vinaigrette, or marinade to add another flavor dimension, the same way you would use an herb or spice. For example, if you want to add cumin flavor to a bean salad, dilute the essential oil in a little olive oil, then toss the olive oil with the salad. Or add a few drops of cinnamon essential oil to melted butter, then use that butter to make cinnamon toast.

You can also dilute essential oils in liquid. Try using the oils to flavor a soup, stew, or consommé. For example, add a drop or two of ginger essential oil to carrot soup, finish a fish stew with a little saffron essential oil, or use the black pepper essential oil to season a consommé. Dilute a few drops of the essential oil in a few ounces of whatever liquid you want to season, then add that seasoned liquid to the rest a little at a time. This will allow you to accurately control the strength of the essential oil in the finished dish.

Each ingredient section includes some tips on how to use essential oils in every-day cooking, and alternative uses for some of the component recipes, such as vinaigrettes, infused oils, and sauces.

Essential oils are not going to replace the fresh ingredients they are distilled from, but as a staple of your pantry they will add new flavor and aromatic dimension to your cooking.

INGREDIENT BASICS

Vegetables, meat, poultry, fish, and dairy products are living things, changeable and often erratic in both quality and internal properties. You may find fish that is one inch thick one week and two inches thick the following week, and you cannot hope to cook both pieces in exactly the same way. Sometimes onions will be tougher and require longer cooking time, or carrots will be more vegetal and may require a pinch of sugar to bring up their sweetness. There are many specific instructions about cooking times, but ultimately it is the ingredients themselves that tell you what to do. For example, if your braised duck seems done after one hour, then it is done, regardless of what the recipe says. It could be that the duck is especially tender, or that your oven is running a bit hot. The converse is true as well, that some things may take longer than the guidelines in the recipe state.

Fruits and vegetables are particularly changeable, depending on time of year, ripe-ness, soil conditions, rainfall patterns, and so forth. For example, lemons might be sweeter one week and tarter the next. This will change the amount of juice needed in a recipe.

The recipes here were created using certain ingredients. You may or may not have the same ingredients available to you. Use your best judgment in making substitutions, and above all choose ingredients that excite you—they are the driving force behind the success of the dishes. If you cannot find good-quality ingredients for a dish that you want to make, choose another recipe that better suits the ingredients at hand.

Keep in mind also that the essential oils are natural ingredients as well and are prone to subtle variation. Taste as you go to make sure that the flavors and aromas are correct.

Salt

Salt is the single most important ingredient in cooking. Used correctly it illuminates the essential flavors of a dish, making them glow from within. I recommend using either *sel gris* (a mineral-rich sea salt from France) or *fine sea salt,* but *kosher salt* is an acceptable substitute. Just avoid *iodized salt,* with its harsh chemical taste. Following are some properties of salt that will be helpful to keep in mind.

Salt draws out moisture. This makes meat denser when salted overnight, as in the Black Pepper–Scented Pork Shoulder Confit (page 154), but it also means that a salad's seasoning will be diluted if the salad is salted too far in advance. You may notice that in some recipes meats and poultry are seasoned and left covered at room temperature for about twenty minutes, especially when being poached or steamed. The reason for this is that the salt is absorbed into the meat and doesn't wash off in the cooking medium. Conversely, in other recipes the salt is sprinkled on meat, poultry, or fish just before sautéing so it fuses with the browned crust, creating a dynamic immediacy of flavor. You will also notice that salt is invariably added to vegetables that are "sweated," that is, cooked until tender without browning. Here salt draws moisture from the vegetables while they are cooking, creating a humid environment so that they are less likely to burn.

Salt modifies the balance of sweetness and acidity in a recipe, bringing out acidity and muting sweetness. In a sauce that is sweet and sour, such as the coffee-fig sauce for pork chops (page 127), salt reduces the sweetness while bringing out the sharpness of the lime juice and vinegar, making the sauce more savory, balanced, and complex. In the Heirloom Tomato and Yellow Doll Watermelon Salad (page 84) salt turns a combination that could be overly sweet into a lively interaction. Even many of the desserts, such as the Prune-Cognac Sorbet (page 181), benefit from a few pinches of salt, which bring out flavors potentially obscured by the sugar. Think of salt as the focus on a camera lens, whose subtle adjustments can transform a blurry image into a clear picture. Salt intensifies flavors that are already present, making the ingredients themselves more vibrant.

Salt that is added progressively, in increments as each ingredient is added, helps to reinforce the individuality of each ingredient. Salt that is added at the end of the cooking process creates a more uniform flavor, where each ingredient gives up some of its individuality to a homogeneous whole. Furthermore, broths, stews, and most sauces (although not reductions, which can overly concentrate the salt) have increased intensity of flavor when they are seasoned throughout the cooking process. Because seasoning with salt is so personal and the ingredients are so changeable, there are no specific amounts of salt in any of the recipes. Salting is always to taste.

Vegetable oils

Fruity olive oil refers to extra virgin olive oil with a fresh, bright flavor and aroma. It is usually made from underripe, or green, olives that are harvested and pressed in late fall to early winter, and it has none of the musty off-flavors found in mass-produced supermarket oils (see Sources, page 201).

Pure olive oil is oil from the second pressing of the olives. It has a lighter flavor than first press (extra virgin) olive oil. For this reason it is used in infusions, where you do not want the olive flavor to dominate. Its higher burning point makes it ideal for sautéing.

The *peanut oil* called for in recipes is refined peanut oil, which is almost flavorless, simply a vehicle for other flavors. Don't use roasted peanut oil, which will taste intensely of peanuts and overwhelm whatever it is used with.

Vinegar

The recipes all call for vinegars with 7 percent acidity (except for rice wine vinegar, which is milder). If the label on your vinegar bottle shows a lower percentage, use more. If the percentage is higher, use less. Trust your instincts—if it seems as though the dish needs more vinegar, then by all means add it.

Buy the best-quality vinegar you can find. Even the finest vinegars are not very expensive (see Sources, page 201).

USEFUL TOOLS

Mandoline

Along with a sharp knife, a Japanese mandoline is an indispensable cutting tool. Many of the recipes call for finely shaved, sliced, diced, or julienned vegetables, and a mandoline makes the work quick and easy. Mandolines are inexpensive and can be purchased in many kitchen supply stores (see Sources, page 201).

Mortar and pestle

A mortar is a heavy bowl, usually stone although occasionally wood. It is used to grind spices, garlic, or herbs (as for pesto). The pestle is the implement that does the grinding. Buy something easily washable and nonporous, such as marble or another stone that will not retain flavors and aromas. To use a mortar and pestle, begin by smashing with an up-and-down motion, and then use a circular motion to grind the ingredient to the desired consistency. Use a mortar and pestle for coarsely ground spices.

Nonreactive pots

Nonreactive refers to pots that do not react with acids, which generally means stainless steel, enamel-lined, or one of the nonstick coatings. It is best to use nonreactive pans for everything you cook, but especially when using acidic foods or liquids such as wine, tomatoes, vinegar, and lemon juice. The combination of acid and aluminum or cast iron can produce off flavors.

Pitchers

Several of the recipes recommend that soups be poured at the table. You can use anything from a "press-style" coffeemaker to water or milk pitchers to pour soup tableside. The pitcher needs to pour easily, and the prettier it is the better, but beyond that just about anything that will hold the appropriate amount will work.

Spice grinder

For finely ground spices, use a coffee grinder. Be sure to clean it well after each use so that the aromas and flavors of the different spices remain distinct, and don't use it for coffee.

COOKING TERMS AND TECHNIQUES

Braise

To braise is to cook slowly in a moist environment. It can refer to a protein that cooks slowly with stock, or a vegetable that cooks gently with butter and its own natural juices. Braised food is almost always covered while it cooks.

Browning and searing

These two terms mean almost but not quite the same thing. *Browning* means cooking at high enough heat to create a brown crust. This usually happens on top of the stove, as with browning meat, although sometimes the oven is used, as when you brown bones. The goal of browning is evenness of color and depth of flavor.

The goal of *searing*, on the other hand, is to rapidly brown and sometimes even blacken the outside of the food. Searing often leads to uneven color, which can be a good thing, as with the brussels sprouts and fennel that accompany the Coriander-Crusted Wild Salmon (page 172).

Charring onions
There are several recipes, especially for stocks, that call for charred onions, which add complexity and subtle smokiness. If you have gas burners, then you can cut peeled yellow onions in half and burn the cut side over an open flame for a few minutes, until mostly blackened. If you have electric burners, you can either put the cut side of the onions directly on burners set to high, or put a piece of aluminum foil on the burner first, and then char the onion on top of the aluminum foil.

Chiffonade
Chiffonade refers to finely sliced herbs and leafy greens. To make a chiffonade of herbs, stack two leaves at a time flat on the cutting board and thinly slice them. Chiffonade is an easy and elegant way to get the truest flavor out of an herb, without bruising the leaves as chopping sometimes does.

Cooling down liquids
To cool down liquids, set a stainless steel mixing bowl into a larger mixing bowl filled with ice and water. Pour the liquid you would like to cool down into the top mixing bowl and stir gently until it is cold. This will cool the liquids down as quickly and efficiently as possible.

Cooling down vegetables
Leafy greens must be cooled down by plunging them into ice water until cold and then draining them; otherwise they will discolor. That technique, however, dilutes the flavor and compromises the texture of other kinds of vegetables, which should be spread out on a plate or sheet pan to cool, then refrigerated if necessary.

Dice
To dice a vegetable, cut it into thin, even slices, then stack the slices and slice them into long strands. Line up the strands lengthwise and slice crosswise to create cubes. Ideally the pieces should all be around the same size.

Julienne

Julienne refers to vegetables that are sliced into thin, even strands. This is generally accomplished by cutting the vegetables into slices first, then stacking the slices in piles of two or three and cutting them into thin strips. For fennel, separate the bulb into individual leaves by cutting out the core and separating the leaves, then slicing each leaf separately. The Japanese mandoline can be very helpful in this process, by either making the initial slices very even, or by using the teeth attachments that come with it to julienne directly. The cut of the julienne sides should be square, which will happen if the cut is the same thickness, usually between one-eighth and one-sixteenth of an inch. This cut allows for even cooking, and it makes the presentation more attractive.

Measurements

Most measurements in these recipes are in volume, but some of them, especially the baking recipes, are in weight, which is a more accurate measurement. Most upscale kitchen supply stores now carry electronic scales for about $30, which make a worthwhile investment. Even when not baking, the weight of an ingredient is still important. For example, onions vary in size from six ounces to twelve ounces or more, so if you use a twelve-ounce onion in a recipe calling for a six-ounce one, you would double the amount called for, which would affect the balance of the dish.

Resting

When meat is cooked, especially over high heat, the juices are naturally drawn to the surface. *Resting* refers to letting the meat sit for a period of time after it is cooked, usually on a plate or in a pan in a warm but not hot place, so that the juices become redistributed throughout the meat. That way when you slice the meat the juices will stay inside the meat to moisten it, instead of running out onto your cutting board.

Straining

Straining soups and sauces makes for a more refined finished product, and it takes only a moment to do. For purees and soups where you want a slightly coarser texture, use a basket strainer. For the more refined sauces and pastry bases, use a fine mesh sieve.

Sweating vegetables (cooking gently)

This technique is an important way to cook all sorts of vegetables, especially onions, to highlight the sweetness and true flavor of a vegetable. Vegetables that are sweated are cooked over low heat in a covered pot with a little bit of fat, usually olive oil or butter. The pot should be heavy-bottomed to avoid any browning, and salt should be added at the beginning to help draw out the moisture. The vegetable should also be stirred occasionally to help it cook evenly.

Transference of unwanted aroma and flavors

The recipes in this book are designed to get you to think about the relationship of aroma and flavor and its importance in cooking. One aspect of this approach is not only to maximize the aromas and flavors that you want, but to minimize those that you do not want. Everything that touches the food, from your hands to knives and containers, should be absolutely clean and odor-free. The cutting board is one of the primary places that can transfer unwanted aromas and flavors. Smell the board before using it to make sure that there are no residual food or soap smells, and then clean the board well after cutting strongly aromatic ingredients, such as onions or rosemary, on it. Cutting boards should also be cleaned with a light bleach solution after any meat, poultry, or fish is cut on them, and then rinsed well. Before using any utensil, pot, or pan, from strainer baskets to spatulas, smell it first to make sure that it is perfectly clean.

Warm water baths

Sometimes, as with a delicate butter sauce, you will want to hold a sauce warm but not hot, or it will break. To do this, heat a pan half filled with water until the water is very warm, then place the container of sauce into the water bath, taking care that the water is not too high, or the sauce container might tip over.

Refreshing

Spearmint
Cucumber
Lime
Orange
Lemon Verbena

Lemon Verbena "Lemonade" (page 60).
OPPOSITE: Mint-Infused Asparagus Soup (page 39).

SPEARMINT~

Spearmint essential oil is produced by steam distillation of the flowering tops of the plants. This pale oil evokes the sharp, green, and powerful herbaceous odor of the crushed herb. Spearmint oil improves with age—one-year-old oils are finer and have a more characteristic minty fragrance than freshly distilled oils. Spearmint blends well with jasmine, basil, grapefruit, and vetiver. Its cheerful scent does wonders to lift a heavy composition, and it is a refreshing addition to bath salts.

Although there are many kinds of mint available, from peppermint to chocolate mint, these recipes have all been developed using spearmint oil. Because of its sweetness and balanced flavor, combined with penetrating aroma, spearmint is the most versatile of the mints, and the one that combines best with other flavors. Look for dark green and vibrant leaves with no bruising or wilting. In addition to fresh mint, there is spearmint essential oil in the Mint Puree (page 42) and the Chocolate-Mint Truffles (page 43). The combination is positively invigorating.

IN THE EVERYDAY KITCHEN: Mix a few drops of spearmint essential oil with hot water and honey to make a delightful tisane, or add a drop or two to a pitcher of iced tea. Add the Mint Puree (page 42) to a pasta or bean salad, or spoon over grilled fish. You can also make basil puree using the same technique.

pictured on page 18

Mint is the highlight of this refreshing herbal blend, even though there's less of it by volume than the other oils because mint has a very intense fragrance. The basil and coriander temper the mint, creating a full scent with a chord of green notes. A comforting aroma with familiar notes makes these bath salts perfect for a long relaxing soak.

1 cup fine sea salt	**5 drops spearmint essential oil**
30 drops coriander essential oil	**20 drops bergamot essential oil**
10 drops basil essential oil	

Place the salt in a bowl, then add the essential oils drop by drop, stirring the mixture with a chopstick to evenly mix the oils with the salt. Pour the fragrant salts into a jar or bottle with a tight-fitting lid. Let the salts sit for a week, allowing the scents to marry and the salts to absorb them. The finished salts should be enough for two baths.

Mint-Infused Asparagus Soup

SERVES 8, pictured on page 37

In this recipe quickly cooked asparagus is blended with mint and crème fraîche to create a vibrant and refreshing soup. A salad of finely shaved raw asparagus is tossed with peppery radish, slightly bitter endive, sweet-tart apple, and a little rice wine vinegar is plated in the center of the soup bowls, and the soup is then poured around it. Recommend to the diners that they stir the soup and salad together. The bright, crunchy vegetables and smooth, fragrant soup create a wonderful interplay of flavors and textures.

Make sure that the asparagus is sweet and tender. The best way to check is to cut off a piece of one and try it. If you do not find that it is good enough to eat raw, then make the salad with only the radish, endive, and mint. You can make the soup ahead of time, but reheat it just before serving or the color and flavor will suffer. You will need a bunch of fresh mint for the recipe.

ASPARAGUS SOUP

4 bunches large asparagus, tough ends trimmed (about 4 pounds)

1 medium yellow onion, peeled and sliced (about 6 ounces unpeeled)

Salt

1 tablespoon unsalted butter

3 cups Vegetable Stock (page 197)

20 large fresh mint leaves

1/4 cup Crème Fraîche (page 200)

ENDIVE, RADISH, AND APPLE SALAD

Reserved asparagus

4 red radishes

9 leaves red endive (or regular endive; just make sure it is not too bitter)

6 fresh mint leaves

1/4 peeled and seeded Granny Smith apple

1 tablespoon rice wine vinegar

Salt and freshly ground black pepper

FOR THE SOUP: Roughly chop three-quarters of the asparagus—peel and reserve the remainder for the salad. In a pot with a tight-fitting lid, cook the onions gently in the butter with salt, covered, until tender. Uncover, add the vegetable stock and more salt, cover, and bring to a boil, then turn down and let simmer for about 10 minutes. Remove the lid, add the chopped asparagus and cook, uncovered, for 3 to 4 minutes, until the asparagus is barely tender and still bright green. Remove from the heat and puree in a blender with the mint leaves and the crème fraîche. Season to taste with salt and, if you are not serving the soup immediately, cool it quickly in an ice bath or it will lose its bright green color and fresh flavor.

FOR THE SALAD: While the onions are cooking, thinly slice the radish and reserved asparagus on a mandoline and put them in a covered mixing bowl in the refrigerator. When you are ready to serve the soup, slice the endive and make a chiffonade of mint, thinly slice the apple crosswise on a mandoline, add them to the other salad ingredients, and season the salad with the rice wine vinegar, salt, and black pepper. Divide the salad evenly among six to eight soup bowls, making a small mound in the center of each bowl.

TO SERVE: Transfer the hot soup to a pitcher, and at the table pour the soup around the salads.

Steamed Halibut Wrapped in Napa Cabbage with Mint

SERVES 8

The halibut is wrapped with mint in napa cabbage leaves that have been blanched, creating little packages that are then steamed and placed on top of a mushroom–quinoa salad with a bright green puree of mint drizzled around the plate. Quinoa is a South American grain, originally grown in the Andes, and in addition to being delicious, it is one of the healthiest grains you can eat. When cooked, it has a firm but yielding texture and the look of large beige caviar.

The napa cabbage here both protects the fish while it cooks and adds another textural element to the dish. Make sure not to overlap the cabbage too much when wrapping the fish. Also, if the plates are warm (but not hot), the mint will be even more aromatic. If you are short on time, you can simply sauté the halibut in pure olive oil and serve it with the same accompaniments.

3 cups water	Eight 5-ounce pieces halibut fillet
Salt and freshly ground black pepper	2 bunches fresh mint
6 ounces quinoa	Marinated Mushrooms (recipe follows)
8 large napa cabbage leaves	

FOR THE QUINOA: Bring the water to a boil, salt lightly, and cook the quinoa until tender but not mushy, about 20 minutes. Taste for salt while it is cooking, adding more as needed. A tiny dot of whiteness in the center of each grain, similar to the center of undercooked pasta, indicates that the quinoa is undercooked. The second that the dot disappears the quinoa is ready. Be sure to taste it frequently as it cooks, because it can go from undercooked to overcooked very rapidly. When the quinoa is ready, strain and discard the cooking liquid and spread the quinoa on a plate to cool.

FOR THE FISH: While the quinoa is cooking, cook the cabbage leaves in a pot of salted, simmering water until they are tender, about 30 seconds, then plunge the leaves into an ice bath to cool. Remove from the ice bath, drain well in a colander, and lay the leaves on paper towels to remove any excess moisture. Trim the sides of the cabbage so they just touch when folded over a piece of fish. Season the fish with salt and black pepper on both sides. Place a piece of cabbage on a plate with the outside of the leaf facing down. Place 2 mint leaves on the cabbage, and then put the fish flesh side down on the mint. Place 2 more mint leaves on top of each fillet. Fold the top and bottom of the cabbage over the fish, then bring the sides over that fold, and then turn the cabbage package over. Repeat for the remaining fillets. Set a steamer over simmering water. Steam the cabbage packages for 10 to 15 minutes, or until the fish is cooked. Check this by opening one or two of the packages enough to see that the fish is opaque but not raw in the center, and firm to the touch.

TO SERVE: While the fish is cooking, toss the quinoa with the marinated mushrooms, including any extra oil and vinegar from the mushrooms. Place a mound of the mixture in the center of the each plate, and then drizzle a tablespoon of the mint puree around. When the fish is ready, place one package on top of each mound of quinoa and mushrooms.

MARINATED MUSHROOMS

1/3 cup pure olive oil

12 ounces meaty mushrooms, such as portobello or abalone, cut into 1/2-inch cubes

Salt and freshly ground black pepper

1/3 cup champagne vinegar

1/3 cup fruity olive oil

Heat the pure olive oil to medium-hot, and then add the mushrooms—you may need to do this in a few batches if your sauté pan is not very large. When the mushrooms are coated in the oil, season them with salt. Cook the mushrooms until browned and tender, remove from heat, and transfer to a plate to cool. Toss the mushrooms with the champagne vinegar and the fruity olive oil, adjusting the seasoning with salt and black pepper.

MINT PUREE

1 cup fresh mint leaves, tightly packed

1/3 cup pure olive oil

2 drops spearmint essential oil

Suspend a basket strainer in a pot of well-salted boiling water. Put the mint leaves in the basket and cook for 5 seconds, then immediately plunge the basket into a bowl filled with ice and water. Stir the leaves to cool them. Drain and squeeze the leaves until they are fairly dry, and then chop them coarsely. Put them in a blender with the pure olive oil and the mint essential oil, then puree for 30 seconds, or until the oil is bright green and the mint finely chopped.

Chocolate-Mint Truffles

MAKES 40 TO 80 TRUFFLES

Here the classic combination of chocolate and mint is invigorated by the intensity of spearmint essential oil, which creates a bright aromatic counterpoint to the darkness of the chocolate. If you do not serve the truffles immediately, store them, well wrapped, in the refrigerator for up to two weeks.

16 ounces bittersweet chocolate, preferably Valrhona

2 cups heavy cream

15 drops spearmint essential oil

1/2 cup unsweetened cocoa powder, preferable Valrhona Manjari

Chop the chocolate into small pieces (the exact size does not matter too much, but try to get them all the same size). Melt the chocolate in a bowl set over barely simmering water. When the chocolate is almost all melted, add the cream and remove from the heat, stirring to combine. Stir in the spearmint essential oil, pour the mixture into a container, and refrigerate until firm, at least 2 hours.

Spread the cocoa powder out on a baking tray. Fill a container with warm water. Scoop out truffles with a melon baller and place them on the baking tray. To make scooping easier, after scooping each truffle, dip the melon baller in the warm water and shake off the excess moisture. If you want, you can roll them in your hands to make evenly round balls.

Gently shake the tray to coat the truffles in cocoa powder, and refrigerate the truffles until they firm up a bit. Serve at room temperature.

CUCUMBER ~

There is no cucumber essential oil, but a *hydrosol* captures cucumber's fresh fragrance. Its simplicity is perfection. It combines beautifully with citrus or herbal hydrosols like rosemary, verbena, and lavender.

Choose firm, crisp cucumbers, preferably in summer when they are at their finest. European cucumbers, which are longer and skinnier, have the best flavor during the off-season. An excessively waxy feel on the outside of the cucumber may mean that it was destined to be stored for an inordinately long time. The addition of the hydrosol to the recipes will intensify the aroma and flavor, but the dishes will also work well without it.

IN THE EVERYDAY KITCHEN: Dilute cucumber hydrosol with an equal amount of water and freeze in ice cube trays. Use the ice cubes to freshen glasses of drinking water. Try adding a little cucumber hydrosol to gazpacho.

CUCUMBER AND ROSEMARY MIST

This simple blend of cucumber and rosemary is fresh and clean, the essence of summer. Cucumber's cool green nature is complemented by the bracing herbal scent of rosemary (you'll find that rosemary hydrosol has none of the sharpness of rosemary essential oil). Spray the mixture on your face or your linens for a delicious pick-me-up, or add a little to a glass of chilled water. It's as close as you can come to drinking an aroma.

1 ounce cucumber hydrosol

1 ounce rosemary hydrosol

Pour hydrosols together in an attractive spray bottle and mix well. Keep in the refrigerator and use within 4 months.

Chilled Cucumber Consommé

SERVES 8

The intensity of cucumber flavor and aroma in this simple recipe is remarkable. This is a clear soup made by adding lemon juice, rice wine vinegar, and salt to cucumber juice. The juicing of the cucumbers alone will make the entire kitchen smell wonderful. If you do not have a vegetable juicer, you can puree the peeled cucumber in a food processor, and then push the liquid through a fine mesh sieve. You may need an extra cucumber using this method, as it will not be as efficient as a juicer.

The soup has a saladlike component in the bowls for textural and flavor contrast, and is poured at the table to maximize the aroma. Toss the salad at the very last minute to keep the salt and acid from drawing the moisture out of the cucumber and diluting the flavor. Alternately, serve the consommé on its own in cups or small glasses as an appetizer or a palate cleanser during a long meal. This recipe requires about eight cucumbers, about seven pounds total.

continued

CUCUMBER CONSOMMÉ

6 cups cucumber juice, skimmed of foam (about 7 cucumbers)

3 tablespoons fresh lemon juice

3 tablespoons cucumber hydrosol

1 tablespoon champagne vinegar

Salt

CUCUMBER, RADISH, AND FENNEL SALAD

2¼ cups peeled, seeded, and finely sliced cucumber (about 1 cucumber)

1½ cups finely shaved fennel

1 cup finely shaved red radish

1 tablespoon plus 1 teaspoon rice wine vinegar

Salt and freshly ground black pepper

FOR THE CONSOMMÉ: Peel the cucumbers and cut them in half lengthwise. Juice them in a vegetable juicer according to the manufacturer's directions and strain the juice through a fine mesh sieve if there is any particulate matter. Combine all ingredients, season to taste with salt, and refrigerate. Make this no more than 6 hours before serving, as it will discolor a bit over time.

FOR THE SALAD: Toss all the vegetables with the rice wine vinegar and season with salt and black pepper.

TO SERVE: Divide the salad evenly among eight chilled bowls, placing a small pile in the center of each. Place the bowls on the table and pour the consommé into each bowl around the salad.

Slow-Cooked Wild Salmon with Marinated Cucumbers

SERVES 8

In this recipe, the salmon is cooked very slowly, so that it becomes incredibly tender and moist, and is served warm but not hot, paired with a cucumber salad and a creamy yogurt-dill sauce. The silkiness of the salmon makes a perfect foil for the clean acidity of the cucumbers and the tangy sauce. The cucumber salad is tossed in a dressing of cucumbers and vinegar to intensify the cucumber flavor, and cucumber is also grated into the yogurt sauce.

The wild king salmon in late spring and early summer, especially salmon from the Pacific Northwest, is milder and sweeter than the later-season fish, but its lower fat content requires gentle cooking. This light dish makes a nice lunch or warm-weather dinner main course.

2 to 3 cucumbers, depending on size

2 tablespoons champagne vinegar

2 tablespoons cucumber hydrosol

1 teaspoon sugar

Salt and freshly ground black pepper

Eight 5-ounce pieces of salmon fillet, skin, excess fat, and bones removed

2 tablespoons pure olive oil

Yogurt-Dill Sauce (recipe follows)

FOR THE CUCUMBER SALAD: Peel the cucumbers and cut into 2-inch pieces. Using a mandoline fitted with a medium serrated blade, julienne the cucumber. Cut only the flesh from the outside, reserving one cup of the soft pulp and seeds for the vinaigrette.

FOR THE VINAIGRETTE: Puree the reserved cup of cucumber pulp in a blender with the champagne vinegar, cucumber hydrosol, sugar, and salt to taste. Pass through a basket strainer and toss with the julienned cucumber, seasoning to taste with salt and black pepper. Refrigerate until needed, up to 4 hours.

FOR THE SALMON: Preheat the oven to 225°F. Brush the salmon with the pure olive oil and season with salt and black pepper on both sides. Place the salmon in a sauté or cast-iron pan (a thick pan is best) with the fat side down and place in the oven. Cook for 10 to 15 minutes, depending on the thickness of the fillet. When done, the top of the salmon will still appear quite rare, but the proteins in the flesh will have set very softly and the fish will separate into moist flakes, especially toward the bottom. Try cooking one piece first and tasting it to see how rare you like it.

TO SERVE: While the salmon is cooking, spread about 1½ ounces of yogurt-dill sauce in the center of each room-temperature plate. Mound about ⅓ cup of marinated cucumbers in the center of the sauce and finish with a salmon fillet on top of the cucumbers.

YOGURT-DILL SAUCE

2 teaspoons minced shallots

½ teaspoon sugar

1 tablespoon plus 1 teaspoon champagne vinegar

1 tablespoon plus 1 teaspoon fresh lemon juice

Salt and freshly ground black pepper

½ cup peeled and grated cucumber

1 cup plain whole-milk yogurt

½ cup Crème Fraîche (page 200)

2 teaspoons chopped fresh dill

Combine the shallots, sugar, champagne vinegar, lemon juice, and some salt in a mixing bowl, and let stand for 20 minutes. Add the remaining ingredients and correct the seasoning. Refrigerate until needed.

Cucumber-Melon Sorbet

MAKES 2 QUARTS

Cucumbers and melons are in the same family, and they combine beautifully. The crisp freshness of the cucumber balances the musky sweetness of the melon, and the aromas of the two are wonderful together. Use the ripest melon you can find.

½ honeydew melon (about 3½ pounds)	3 tablespoons cucumber hydrosol
4 cucumbers (about 3½ pounds)	3 tablespoons fresh lemon juice
1 cup Simple Syrup (page 200)	Salt

Peel, seed, and coarsely chop the melon. Peel and chop the cucumber. Puree the two together in a blender in batches, using a little simple syrup with each batch. Pass the mixture through a fine mesh sieve and add the cucumber hydrosol, lemon juice, and salt. Taste the sorbet base and season with more simple syrup, lemon juice, or a pinch of salt, as needed. Freeze in a sorbet maker according to the manufacturer's instructions.

LIME~

The lime is a thorny, bushy evergreen tree with handsome dark green leaves so fragrant that they have been used to perfume the water in finger bowls. The rind of the fruit is pressed to yield lime essential oil, a greenish liquid that captures the rind's characteristic fresh, sweet odor. Used moderately, the oil is a good choice to finish off blends that are too sweet or floral. Try blending it with angelica, nutmeg, and neroli.

From the cook's perspective, lime is more tart than other citruses, with the most angular, penetrating aroma. Where lemon caresses and joins other flavors, lime cuts through and defines them. For example, a few drops of lemon juice will add gentle acidity to a vinaigrette or sauce but remain in the background, while the same amount of lime juice will immediately announce its presence. Limes should be firm, with a sharp fragrance that is quick to make itself known. The recipes use both the juice and zest of the lime, as well as its essential oil. Buy cold-pressed lime peel essential oil, which has an extraordinary flavor and aroma.

IN THE EVERYDAY KITCHEN: Mix a little lime essential oil with lime juice, Simple Syrup (page 200), and sparkling mineral water for a vibrant and refreshing drink. Use a few drops instead of lime zest when you want to infuse a sauce with citrus flavor. Add a little fruity olive oil to the Lime Vinaigrette (page 51) to temper its acidity, then use it as a marinade for baked or grilled chicken.

LIME AND FIR DIFFUSER OR BATH OIL

A diffuser is a lovely way to circulate scent through a room. A bowl of water warmed by a candle works fine in a small room. You can fill ceramic rings with oil and place them on top of a lightbulb. When the heat reaches the oil it will slowly diffuse the scent. You can also add this oil straight to your bath after the tub is full and you are in it (remember that hot water disperses essential oils). The bath oil clings to you when you get out of the water, leaving you subtly perfumed.

Fir oil is sweet and jamlike and reminds us of the smell of clean forest air. Bitter orange, with its slight floral undertone, is complemented by similar notes in the lavender essential oil and combines beautifully with the dryness of the fir. The addition of lime echoes the fir's outdoorsy green note.

5 milliliters fir essential oil

2 milliliters lime essential oil

1 milliliters bitter orange essential oil

2 millileters lavender essential oil

Combine the essential oils in a small bottle, preferably one with a dropper cap. Add a dropperful to your diffuser or bath.

Tuna-Tomato Tartare with Lime Vinaigrette

SERVES 8

This is a fun dish, both to serve and to eat. The diced tomato and tuna that are tossed together with lime vinaigrette look very similar, so the first bite is a surprise. Be sure to use bright-red tuna from the meaty loin rather than the fatty belly, fully ripe tomatoes, and to dice them the exact same size. Cut small (¼-inch) dice so that it is almost impossible to tell the difference between the two. Keep the tomatoes and tuna separate until you are ready to finish the dish, or the acid in the tomatoes will cook the tuna.

LIME VINAIGRETTE

Salt

2 tablespoons plus 2 teaspoons fresh lime juice

¼ cup pure olive oil

25 drops lime essential oil

TARTARE

11 ounces peeled, seeded, diced tomato (about 6 medium tomatoes)

1 pound tuna, diced

2 tablespoons minced fresh hives

Salt and freshly ground black pepper

FOR THE LIME VINAIGRETTE: Dissolve a little salt in the lime juice, then whisk in the olive oil and the lime essential oil. Adjust seasoning as needed.

For the diced tomato, cut a small "x" in the bottom of each tomato and cook in boiling water for 10 to 15 seconds, or until the skins loosen. Remove the tomatoes to a plate to cool, then peel and stem them. Cut the tomatoes into quarters and remove the seeds (save the pulp and juice for another use). Cut the remaining firm flesh into small dice the same size as the tuna.

TO SERVE: Combine the tomatoes, tuna, and chives in a mixing bowl. Add some of the vinaigrette and season with salt and black pepper. Adjust the seasoning, adding more vinaigrette if necessary. Divide among eight plates.

Duck Legs Braised
with Red Wine and Lime

SERVES 8

This is a classic French coq au vin with a twist. Instead of the mushrooms, pearl onions, and the traditional richness of coq au vin (chicken braised in red wine), the duck, braised in medium- to full-bodied wine, is balanced with lime juice, lime essential oil, cilantro, and chile, making a dynamic contrast of sweet, sour, and spicy. The duck is cooked with onions that are later pureed with the braising liquid and aromatics to make a smooth sauce without using any fat. You can make the duck a day or two ahead of time and reheat it in its cooking liquid at 250°F for fifteen to twenty minutes, or until the duck is hot.

DUCK

Zest of 3 limes

8 medium yellow onions (about 3 pounds), peeled and thinly sliced

Salt and freshly ground black pepper

3 tablespoons pure olive oil

1 tablespoon plus 1 teaspoon minced serrano chile

8 duck legs

2 cups red wine, such as merlot or cabernet

3/4 cup water

ONION-LIME SAUCE

1 cup reserved cooked onions

1½ cups reserved braising liquid

1 tablespoon plus 1 teaspoon fresh lime juice

2 tablespoons chopped fresh cilantro

10 drops lime essential oil

Salt

Minced serrano chile, as desired

FOR THE DUCK: To make the lime zest, use a sharp knife or a peeler to remove the peel, and then with a knife remove as much of the white pith from the inside of the peel as possible. Cut the peel lengthwise into thin julienne strips.

In a pot with a tight-fitting lid, cook the onions gently with salt in 1 tablespoon of the olive oil, covered, until tender. Stir in the lime zest and serrano chile.

While the onions are cooking, season the duck legs on both sides with salt and black pepper, then sear them in the remaining 2 tablespoons olive oil. Cook the leg skin side first over medium heat until the skin is golden brown, then turn the legs and cook on the flesh side for 30 seconds only.

Place the legs on top of the onions and add the red wine and water. Bring to a boil, cover, and then place in a 250°F oven for 1½ to 2 hours, or until the duck is tender but still retains discernable texture.

Remove the duck, cool on a plate, cover, and refrigerate. Strain the onions and reserve the liquid—use them both while they are still hot to make the onion-lime sauce.

FOR THE ONION-LIME SAUCE: In a blender, puree all of the ingredients except the serrano chile until smooth. Taste the sauce and, if you want it spicier, add a bit of raw minced chile and reblend. Strain the sauce through a basket strainer and adjust the seasoning as necessary with salt and lime juice—it should be quite bright. If you are making the duck ahead of time, cool and reserve the sauce and leftover onions separately, and reserve the braising liquid and duck in the same container.

TO SERVE: Warm the duck legs with the remaining braising liquid in a 250°F oven until hot. While the duck is in the oven, heat the remaining onions and the onion-lime sauce separately.

In warm soup plates, mound a pile of onions in the center. Sauce around with the onion-lime sauce and place a duck leg on top of the onions.

Caramel-Lime Sauce

MAKES 3 CUPS

This caramel sauce is made with water instead of cream or butter, which makes the flavors especially vibrant. Fresh lime juice and lime essential oil balance the sweetness of the caramel, and the resulting sauce is a great accompaniment to apple tarts, drizzled on ice cream, or tossed with sautéed pears or cherries. It will keep refrigerated for up to one month.

2 cups sugar	25 drops lime essential oil
2 cups water	Salt
2 tablespoons fresh lime juice	

Dissolve the sugar and ¾ cup of water in a heavy, nonreactive pot, preferably with high sides. Cook over medium-high heat for about 10 minutes, until the mixture turns a deep brown color and you can smell the caramelized sugar.

Off the heat, carefully whisk in the remaining 1¼ cups water. Return to the heat and bring to a boil for 15 to 20 seconds, until the caramel is completely dissolved. Remove from the heat, let cool slightly, and transfer to a heat-resistant container. Add the lime juice, lime essential oil, and salt, and stir to dissolve. Cool and refrigerate until needed.

ORANGE~

Sweet orange essential oil, with a fresh odor reminiscent of the scratched peel, is used in perfumery as a vibrant, if simple, *top note*. Bitter orange essential oil, distilled from the peel of the fruit, is dry and delicate. Blood orange essential oil has a rich orange aroma with overtones of raspberry and strawberry.

From a cook's perspective, orange works beautifully with a wide range of ingredients, from anise to spicy greens, pork, veal, chicken, game, and seafood. Its round, sweet perfume and flavor balance out bitter, spicy, sour, or salty flavors. Both the juice and zest of the orange are indispensable accent notes that add interest and lift to other flavors, in the way candied orange sets off the Coffee-Date Ice Cream with Candied Orange (page 128). Blood orange is exotic, at once familiar and exciting, with its beautiful light to deep crimson color and bracing acidity. For all kinds of oranges, including blood oranges, look for heavy fruit with firm, tight skin. Flavor varies according to variety and season, but, like all citrus, it is best in winter.

IN THE EVERYDAY KITCHEN: Add a little sweet orange essential oil to intensify the flavor and aroma whenever you cook with orange. Sorbets, ice cream, vinaigrettes, and sauces are a few possibilities. Use either the Blood Orange Vinaigrette (page 86) or the Bitter Orange Vinaigrette (page 58) to dress a vegetable or spinach salad. Because the essential oil is pressed from the rind, you can use it to season a sauce or batter instead of using fresh zest.

In these cheerful, floral bath salts, the sweetness of ylang-ylang and orange is tempered by the green leafy aroma of geranium. All three of these oils are known for their antidepressant qualities.

1 cup fine sea salt

30 drops geranium essential oil

10 drops sweet orange essential oil

10 drops ylang-ylang "extra" essential oil

Place the salt in a bowl, then add the oils drop by drop, stirring the mixture with a chopstick to evenly combine the oils with the salt. Pour the fragrant salts into a jar or bottle with a tight-fitting lid. Let the salts sit for a week, allowing the scents to marry and the salts to absorb them. The finished salts should be enough for two baths.

Blood Orange, Fennel, and Avocado Salad

SERVES 8

This colorful salad is like the warmth of bright sunshine amid winter's dreariness. It has varied textures, lively flavors, and a vinaigrette made with blood orange juice and a few drops of blood orange essential oil. If the arugula leaves are very large, coarsely chop them into bite-size pieces to make it possible to taste the different elements in each bite.

4 cups shaved fennel (about 3 large bulbs)

1½ cups blood orange segments (about 6 oranges)

6 cups young arugula

Blood Orange Vinaigrette (page 56)

Salt and freshly ground black pepper

4 avocados, peeled and sliced

Toss the fennel, blood orange segments, and arugula with the blood orange vinaigrette, salt, and black pepper.

continued

TO SERVE: Fan out half an avocado to one side of each plate. Season with salt and black pepper. Divide the salad evenly among the plates, placing it next to and slightly overlapping the avocado. Serve immediately.

BLOOD ORANGE VINAIGRETTE

Salt

¼ cup fresh blood orange juice

1 teaspoon champagne vinegar

¼ cup fruity olive oil

⅜ teaspoon blood orange essential oil

White pepper

In a mixing bowl, dissolve some salt in the blood orange juice and champagne vinegar. Whisk in the olive oil and blood orange essential oil and season with salt and white pepper. If the blood orange juice is very sweet, add a few drops more champagne vinegar to balance the vinaigrette.

Pork Loin Paillards with Spicy Orange-Mint Compote

SERVES 8

A *paillard* is the French name for a piece of meat that has been pounded very thin before being sautéed. The recipe instructs you how to prepare the paillards, but you could ask your butcher to prepare them for you. In this recipe, the paillard is cooked quickly and laid over a bed of orange-scented grilled radicchio, then dressed with a chunky sauce that is a cross between a compote and a vinaigrette. The orange and mint flavors with the pork are delightful, and the bitterness of the radicchio adds a refreshing accent. The compote can be made the day before and refrigerated, but let it come to room temperature before you serve the dish.

1 head radicchio

½ cup pure olive oil

Salt and freshly ground black pepper

6 to 8 pieces of pork loin, about 4 to 5 ounces each

Spicy Orange–Mint Compote (recipe follows)

Slice the radicchio into quarters and toss with 2 tablespoons of the pure olive oil. Season them with salt and pepper. Allow a cast-iron skillet to reach medium-high heat, and then grill the radicchio for 2 minutes on all three sides, starting with the two cut sides and finishing with the uncut side. They should be somewhat charred but not burned, tender while retaining their texture. Remove to a plate to cool, and then when cool, discard the core, and cut each piece crosswise into julienne strips.

Slice the pieces of pork almost in half (against the grain) so that they open like a book. Using a mallet, pound them to an even ¼-inch thickness. They will be quite large, so you will probably need a few sauté pans to cook them in, and a plate set in a 150°F oven to hold momentarily the first pieces that you cook while you finish the remainder. Season the pork with salt and pepper and cook over high heat in the remaining 6 tablespoons olive oil, about 1 minute on each side.

TO SERVE: Drain the liquid from the compote, toss it with the radicchio, and season with salt and pepper. Put a thin layer of radicchio on each dinner plate and top with a piece of pork (the paillards should cover most of the plate). Stir the mint into the compote and use the mixture to dress each piece of pork. Serve immediately.

SPICY ORANGE-MINT COMPOTE

1 cup orange segments, all white pith removed, cut into ¼-inch pieces

¼ cup fresh orange juice

2 tablespoons rice wine vinegar

¼ cup fruity olive oil

2 teaspoons minced serrano chile

¼ cup minced fennel

½ teaspoon sweet orange essential oil

Salt

10 leaves fresh mint

Combine all of the ingredients except the mint. Make a chiffonade of the mint and add just before serving.

Flageolet, Tomato, and Basil Salad

SERVES 8

This bright summer salad can be served as a first course or as part of a buffet. The flageolets—small, light green dried beans from France—are combined with chopped tomatoes, basil, and bitter orange vinaigrette. Although essential oil from the bitter orange is used in the vinaigrette, the vinaigrette itself is elegant, not at all bitter. You will need to soak the beans for one day before cooking them. You can cook the beans ahead of time and store them in their cooking liquid in the refrigerator for a day or two, draining just before making the salad. Chop the tomatoes, tear the basil, and toss the salad at the last minute. If you cannot find flageolet beans, small white beans make a fine substitute.

2 cups flageolet beans

Salt and freshly ground black pepper

1 bunch fresh basil

7 medium tomatoes (about 2½ pounds)

Bitter Orange Vinaigrette (recipe follows)

Cover the beans with water and soak them in the refrigerator overnight. The next day, drain them, put them in a pot, and cover with fresh water. Cook partially covered, for about 1½ hours, stirring occasionally, until tender. Add salt halfway through. When the beans are done, remove them from the heat and taste for salt. If they need more, add salt to the water, stir to dissolve, and taste the beans again in about 5 minutes. Cool the beans in their cooking liquid.

Drain the beans and place them in a mixing bowl. Tear the basil leaves into bite-size pieces and put them in the bowl on top of the beans. Core the tomatoes, cut them in sixths, then cut each sixth in three. Add the tomatoes to the bowl, season with salt and black pepper, and pour in half of the vinaigrette. Mix, taste, and add more vinaigrette, salt, or pepper as needed. Serve immediately.

BITTER ORANGE VINAIGRETTE

2 tablespoons fresh orange juice

1 tablespoon fresh lemon juice

1 tablespoon fresh lime juice

Salt

½ cup fruity olive oil

½ teaspoon bitter orange essential oil

Combine the orange juice, lemon juice, and lime juice in a mixing bowl. Dissolve some salt in the mixture and stir in the olive oil and the bitter orange essential oil. Season with salt.

LEMON VERBENA ~

The stalks and leaves of the lemon verbena plant render only a small amount of oil, which causes this essential oil to be quite costly. People often substitute the harsher lemongrass oil, but lemon verbena cannot be matched for its suave and delicate aroma. The intoxicating scent is similar to sweet lemon, but greener and more complex. Unlike citrus essential oils, it is a *middle note* and participates in the evolution of perfume alongside the floral notes. Lemon verbena is known for its ability to calm tension, refresh, and relax. It blends well with citruses, rose, ylang-ylang, geranium, and frankincense

The food recipes use fresh lemon verbena rather than the essential oil. Lemon verbena grows only in the summer, and it is a vibrant plant that grows easily and quickly in just about any garden setting. When you buy lemon verbena, look for forest green leaves with no browning, and an ethereal citruslike aroma.

IN THE EVERYDAY KITCHEN: Dry fresh lemon verbena leaves by spreading them out on a baking sheet, then leaving in a warm place for 2 to 3 days, until completely dry. Store in a container with a tight-fitting lid, and use the leaves to make tea. Dilute the Lemon Verbena Syrup (page 60) with water and lemon juice and freeze it into a granita or sorbet. The Lemon Verbena Butter (page 63) is great for sautéing fish or vegetables, especially peas, or use it instead of clarified butter to make a hollandaise sauce for fish.

LEMON VERBENA–LAVENDER MIST

Lemon verbena mist is quite refreshing and feels wonderful sprayed on your face directly from the refrigerator in a hot day. The slightly floral lemon scent of verbena marries beautifully with the herbal and floral nuances in the rosemary and lavender. This is the kind of scent that is light and cheerful enough to become a daily ritual. You can also mist it over your pillowcases for a relaxing sleep.

10 milliliters verbena hydrosol

2¹/₂ milliliters lavender hydrosol

2¹/₂ milliliters rosemary hydrosol

Pour all three hydrosols into a spray bottle and refrigerate. It is best used within four months.

Lemon Verbena "Lemonade"

SERVES 6 TO 8, pictured on page 36

This is wonderful drink to sip on a hot day—tart, sweet, and perfumed with the unmistakable aroma of lemon verbena.

LEMON VERBENA SYRUP

6 cups water

4 cups fresh lemon verbena leaves, lightly packed

²/₃ cup sugar

LEMONADE:

2 cups cold lemon verbena syrup

6 cups cold sparkling mineral water

2 tablespoons fresh lemon juice

FOR THE LEMON VERBENA SYRUP: Bring the water to a boil. Have a bowl of ice water and a small basket strainer ready. Cook the verbena in the boiling water for about 30 seconds, or until tender. Strain the verbena, reserving both the verbena and the cooking water. Plunge the verbena into the ice water, suspended in the strainer basket so that no ice cubes get into the verbena. Stir the leaves to cool quickly, remove from the water, and squeeze out the excess moisture.

Dissolve the sugar in the cooking liquid and cool in an ice bath. Measure, and add water if necessary to bring to two cups. Puree the liquid and verbena together in a blender for 30 seconds. Strain through a fine mesh sieve and refrigerate. The syrup will oxidize, so make it the day that you intend to drink it.

TO SERVE: Combine the syrup with the mineral water and lemon juice and pour into tall glasses.

Strawberry-Verbena Granita

SERVES 6 TO 8

Strawberries and lemon verbena pair well in this granita, both being intensely floral and perfumed. The delicate granita is served with a thick, vibrant strawberry-verbena sauce and lightly sweetened yogurt, which adds a tangy, creamy counterpoint to this study in textures and temperatures. Although almost everything, even desserts, benefits from a pinch of salt, strawberries are the exception—any salt will only serve to dull their vibrancy.

STRAWBERRY-VERBENA GRANITA

1½ pounds stemmed and quartered strawberries (about 4½ cups)

3 tablespoons plus 1 teaspoon sugar

2 tablespoons minced fresh lemon verbena leaves

2 teaspoons fresh lime juice

¾ cup water

SWEETENED YOGURT

1 tablespoon plus 1 teaspoon sugar

1 cup plain whole-milk yogurt

FOR THE GRANITA: Mix the strawberries, 3 tablespoons sugar, and verbena in a mixing bowl. Cover and refrigerate for 3 to 6 hours, stirring occasionally.

In a blender, puree the strawberries, along with the accumulated juices. If the verbena flavor does not seem strong enough, add a few leaves of verbena, puree, and taste again. Repeat until the strawberry-verbena flavor is balanced. Pass the mixture through a fine mesh sieve and add the lime juice. Season with more lime or sugar, as necessary.

Reserve 1 cup of the strawberry puree for the sauce, and add the water and the 1 teaspoon sugar to the remaining puree. Taste and, if it does not seem sweet enough, add more sugar. Pour into a shallow pan and place it in the freezer for at least 6 hours.

FOR THE SWEETENED YOGURT: Mix the sugar and yogurt together and reserve.

TO SERVE: Put 2 tablespoons of the yogurt in the center of each bowl, and spoon 2 tablespoons of the reserved strawberry-verbena sauce around the yogurt. Using a fork, scrape the frozen strawberry-verbena mixture vigorously to create the granita. Mound a few tablespoons of granita on top of the yogurt and serve immediately.

Veal Tenderloin Slow Cooked in Lemon Verbena Butter

SERVES 8

This dish combines meltingly tender veal with a fragrant sauté of haricots verts, almonds, and lemon verbena. While it is normal to cook prime cuts such as the tenderloin over very high temperature, they actually benefit a great deal from slow cooking. Here the caramelized flavor that comes from browning is replaced by the floral scent of lemon verbena. The slow cooking allows the meat to cook evenly, turning it a diffuse pink all the way through. The proteins also set more softly, making the meat more tender.

Haricots verts is the French term for green beans, but in this country it has come to mean a particular small, tender variety of green bean. If you cannot find them, substitute regular green beans, but choose the smallest available, and cut them in half lengthwise.

¼ cup sliced almonds	Salt and freshly ground black pepper
¼ cup Verbena Butter (recipe follows)	¾ pound haricots verts, stems trimmed
Two 1¼-pound pieces of veal tenderloin, trimmed of all fat and silver connective tissue	1 tablespoon minced fresh lemon verbena leaves

Toast the almonds at 300°F for about 15 minutes, stirring occasionally. Cool. Leave the oven on.

Heat 2 tablespoons of the verbena butter in an ovenproof sauté pan over low heat. Season the veal with salt and black pepper and cook the veal very slowly, turning it after 2 minutes on all sides. Do not let the butter bubble vigorously. If it does, it is cooking too fast. Transfer the sauté pan to the oven, and turn the veal every few minutes until it is medium rare to medium, 15 to 20 minutes. (Because it is cooking so slowly, it will still feel very soft even when sufficiently cooked.) Remove the veal to a plate and let it rest. Discard the cooking fat and wipe out the pan.

While the veal is resting, bring about a quart of well-salted water to a boil. Cook the beans until they are just tender, drain, and add them to the sauté pan with the remaining 2 tablespoons verbena butter, minced verbena, almonds, salt, and black pepper. Cook them gently over medium-low heat for 1 to 2 minutes, until the beans have absorbed the flavor of the verbena. Adjust the seasoning as necessary.

TO SERVE: Slice the veal into thick slices and arrange on one side of each plate. Divide the beans evenly among the plates, putting them next to the veal. Serve immediately.

LEMON VERBENA BUTTER
8 ounces (2 sticks) unsalted butter, cut in cubes
$1/2$ stalk thinly sliced fresh lemongrass
$1/3$ cup chopped fresh lemon verbena leaves
Salt

Cook the butter and lemongrass slowly, skimming often, until the butter is clarified. Add the chopped verbena and a pinch of salt, cook for another 10 minutes, then hold the mixture in a warm place for another 15 minutes. Strain the butter through a fine mesh sieve, pressing the solids to extract all of the verbena flavor. (This will make a little more than you need for the veal. Store in a covered container, refrigerated, for up to 1 month.)

Herbal

Rosemary
Tarragon
Perilla (Shiso)
Lavender

Lavender Shortbread Cookies (page 89).

OPPOSITE: Jasmine-Steamed Chicken Breast (page 112).

ROSEMARY ~

Rosemary essential oil, distilled from the flowering tops and leaves of the plant, has a sharp, penetrating, medicinal aroma and functions as a *top note*. The absolute, a *base note,* is rounded, warm, and somewhat floral. This symbol of remembrance invigorates the mind and blends well with lime, ginger, geranium, and cedarwood.

Although for fragrance making the rosemary essential oil is quite nice, for cooking purposes you can make an infused oil that is lighter, fresher, and more versatile. Made in large batches, it will last for months in your refrigerator, and it combines well with almost every kind of meat and fish, as well as potatoes, white beans, celery, and many other foods. Look for rosemary that has bright green leaves without any browning, a firm texture, and a strong aroma.

IN THE EVERYDAY KITCHEN: Try tossing pasta with rosemary oil, then saucing it with quickly cooked fresh tomatoes. When sautéing a steak, add a few sprigs of rosemary to the pan so the meat will be suffused with its flavor. Use the Rosemary-Infused Oil (page 70) to sauté vegetables, or as a base for a vinaigrette, marinade, or mayonnaise.

ROSEMARY COLOGNE SPRAY

The creation of the original eau de cologne has been credited to Gian Paolo Feminis, an Italian barber in Cologne, Germany, in 1690. He gave the formula to another member of the family, Giovanni Maria Farina, who began making it (with some modifications) in Paris in 1732, where it continued to be made for over a hundred years. This refreshing toilet water is made with grape alcohol, which retains the fruity scent of the grape. Traditionally, the citrus aromas—bergamot, neroli, litsea cubeba, orange—are balanced with the fresh herbal notes of lavender, rosemary, and thyme. This formula is an example of the "less is more" principle, because adding too many herbal essences will mar the beauty of the blend. This cologne is slightly sweet from the rosemary absolute and refreshing and light from the variety of citruses. It can be worn by either sex.

30 milliliters grape alcohol

10 drops rosemary absolute

20 drops benzoin resin

5 drops lavender absolute

20 drops neroli essential oil

1 drop litsea cubeba essential oil

20 drops bitter orange essential oil

20 drops bergamot essential oil

Pour the grape alcohol into a beaker, measuring cup, or small glass. Drop in the essences, beginning with the rosemary absolute, and stir with a stirring stick to mix. Pour the mixture into a bottle with a secure lid and let the fragrances marry for at least a week. Before using, strain the mixture through a plastic coffee filter fitted with unbleached paper. After filtration, this cologne will be deep green and bright like a gemstone. Decant into a spray bottle.

Sweet Onion–Rosemary Soup

SERVES 8

This is a comforting soup to ward off the cold in winter. The sweetness of the onions and garlic combines with the smokiness of bacon and the uplifting aromas of rosemary, reinforced with a drizzle of rosemary-infused oil just before serving. The recipe for rosemary oil makes far more than you will use for this dish, but it is so versatile that the chances are that it will become a staple in your refrigerator, where it will keep for months. It is also used in the two other rosemary recipes. You will need to make the rosemary oil four days in advance.

SWEET ONION-ROSEMARY SOUP

4 tablespoons (½ stick) unsalted butter

4½ cups peeled and sliced yellow onions (2 to 4 onions, depending on size)

6 cloves garlic, peeled and sliced

1 tablespoon minced fresh rosemary

8 ounces diced bacon

Salt and freshly ground black pepper

6 cups Chicken Stock (page 199)

½ cup Rosemary-Infused Oil (recipe follows)

Melt the butter in a nonreactive pot over low heat and add the onions, garlic, rosemary, and bacon. Add salt and cook, covered, until the onions are tender.

Add the chicken stock and some salt, bring to a boil, and then turn down to a simmer. Cook for about 45 minutes, until everything is very soft. Puree in a blender and pass through a soup strainer. Season to taste with salt and black pepper. If you are making the soup ahead of time, cool it down quickly in a pot set into an ice bath, and then refrigerate it covered.

TO SERVE: Heat the soup and ladle into bowls. Drizzle one tablespoon of rosemary oil over each bowl.

ROSEMARY-INFUSED OIL

3 bunches (about 4½ ounces) fresh rosemary

6 cups pure olive oil

Coarsely chop the rosemary, and blend the rosemary and oil together in a food processor or blender for 45 seconds. In a nonreactive pot, heat the oil slightly, until warm but not hot (around 130°F). Let the oil cool down at room temperature and transfer it to a sealed container. Refrigerate the oil for four days, then reheat until warm. Reblend in a food processor or blender for 30 seconds and then strain through a piece of cheesecloth. Refrigerate the oil in a sealed container if not using immediately—it will keep well in the refrigerator for 2 months or more.

Monkfish Roasted on a Bed of Rosemary

Monkfish is a meaty, white-fleshed fish, sometimes called poor man's lobster because of its similarity in texture. This is a wonderful way to cook monkfish, searing it briefly and then roasting it on top of spears of rosemary. The rosemary transforms the monkfish, infusing each bite with aromatic flavor. While it seems at first that the rosemary might be too strong, it mellows as it cooks, its flavor fusing with the cooking juices of the fish while its perfume fills the kitchen. It is important to cook the monkfish on the bone in this recipe because it allows for a longer cooking time and keeps the fish moist. Order your fish ahead of time from your fishmonger, and you shouldn't have a problem getting it on the bone. You will need to soak the beans the day before making the dish. If you do not have time to cook the beans, you can substitute good-quality canned cannellini beans. Mix the liquid in the can with two parts Vegetable Stock (page 197) for the bean cooking liquid.

WHITE BEANS

1 cup white beans

1 yellow onion, peeled and halved

1 carrot, peeled and sliced

5 sprigs fresh thyme

10 peppercorns

Salt

MONKFISH

1 1/2 cups leeks, white and light green parts only, sliced crosswise in 1/4-inch pieces

2 tablespoons plus 1 teaspoon pure olive oil

Salt and freshly ground black pepper

Cooked white beans

1 cup white bean cooking liquid

Two 4-pound monkfish tails, trimmed of all skin and dark fat but left on the bone (your fishmonger will do this for you)

1 large bunch fresh rosemary

8 cups baby spinach

Fresh lemon juice to taste

1/3 cup Rosemary-Infused Oil (page 70)

continued

FOR THE BEANS: Soak the beans in cold water in the refrigerator overnight. The following day, drain the beans, then place them in a large pot and cover them with 1 inch of fresh water. Char one half of the onion (see page 32) and thinly slice the other. Wrap the carrot, onion, thyme, and peppercorns in cheesecloth, and place them in the pot with the beans. Simmer until the beans are tender, about 1½ hours, adding salt about halfway through. When the beans are cooked, take them off of the heat and season the water to taste with salt. The beans will continue to absorb the seasoning while they sit. Remove the aromatics and reserve the beans in their cooking liquid.

FOR THE MONKFISH: Cook the leeks in 1 teaspoon of the olive oil in a covered pot with a little salt until tender. If they become too dry, add a splash of water to moisten them. When they are tender, add the beans and the 1 cup of bean cooking liquid. Remove from the heat.

Preheat oven to 300°F. Season the monkfish all over with salt and black pepper, and sear over high heat in the remaining olive oil in a heavy sauté or cast-iron pan. Meanwhile, lay out the rosemary on a roasting or baking pan. When the monkfish is seared on all sides, set the tails on the rosemary, transfer to the oven, and roast until done, 10 to 15 minutes, depending on the size of the fish. Turn the fish every few minutes, and don't be afraid to use a paring knife to check the doneness. When the fish is just cooked through, it will be solid white in color, not transluscent. Remove the fish to a cutting board.

While the fish is in the oven, add the spinach to the pot with the beans and leeks, and turn the heat to medium-high until the spinach is cooked. Off the heat, season with lemon juice (it should take 1 to 2 tablespoons), salt, and pepper to taste.

TO SERVE: Divide the mixture of beans, spinach, and leeks (including the liquid) among eight warm plates. Drizzle a scant tablespoon of the rosemary oil around each vegetable mixture. Fillet the monkfish by running a knife between the meat and the bone on each side. Slice each loin into thick pieces, and place the fish on top of the vegetable/bean mixture.

Lamb Loin Poached in Rosemary Oil with Crushed Potatoes

SERVES 8

At first glance, the idea of poaching meat in oil may seem strange, but it provides a perfect environment for slow, even cooking that makes each piece perfectly moist and flavorful. The oil will not completely penetrate the lamb, instead staying closer to the surface, so the marriage of herb and meat is a harmonious one, rather than one dominating the other. Make a double batch of the Rosemary-Infused Oil (page 70) to ensure you have enough, and when cooking the lamb, use an oil thermometer to measure the temperature.

The crushed potatoes is a versatile side dish. Because it is comprised only of potatoes and olive oil, use the best quality you can find of each and be careful not to overmix. The olive vinaigrette works equally well with fish preparations.

CRUSHED YUKON GOLD POTATOES

4 pounds Yukon gold potatoes

Salt and freshly ground black pepper

2/3 cup fruity olive oil

2 ounces Rosemary-Infused Oil (page 70)

LAMB

Three 1-pound pieces of lamb loin, trimmed of any fat or silver skin (your butcher should do this for you)

Salt and freshly ground black pepper

1 to 2 quarts Rosemary-Infused Oil (page 70), depending on the shape of your pot

Olive Vinaigrette (page 74)

FOR THE POTATOES: Peel the potatoes and cut them into quarters. Put them in a large pot in generously salted cold water and bring to a simmer. Cook until tender, a tiny bit more than if you were going to eat them whole, but not enough that they lose their integrity. Drain them well, rinse the cooking pot, and put the cooked potatoes back in the pot. Add the olive oil and the rosemary oil, and using a fork crush the potatoes and incorporate the oils. Do not overmix: The potatoes should have lots of potato texture. Taste for seasoning, and add salt and black pepper as necessary. You can make the potatoes up to 1 hour ahead and hold in a covered container set in a warm water bath.

continued

FOR THE LAMB: While the potatoes are cooking, season the lamb with salt and pepper and let stand at room temperature, loosely covered, for 20 minutes. Meanwhile, heat the rosemary oil to 130°F (very warm but not hot) in a pot large enough to hold the lamb. Carefully lower the lamb into the oil. Cook the lamb until it is medium rare to medium, a juicy diffused pink all the way through, about 15 minutes. Move the pieces around every few minutes so they cook evenly. When they are cooked, remove them to a plate and let them stand.

TO SERVE: Put a pile of the potatoes in the center of each plate and drizzle olive vinaigrette around the potatoes. Slice the lamb and fan the slices over the potatoes.

OLIVE VINAIGRETTE

½ cup pitted black olives, preferably Niçoise

2 tablespoons fresh lemon juice

2 tablespoons sherry vinegar

1 teaspoon red wine vinegar

1 cup fruity olive oil

Salt

Put the olives, lemon juice, and vinegars in a blender. Turn the blender on medium-high and slowly drizzle in the olive oil. Taste and add salt if needed.

TARRAGON~

Sweet and spicy tarragon has an aniselike scent. This pale yellow-green *top note* contributes a sweet, herbal, and green aroma to the beginning of any blend. Tarragon blends well with galbanum, lavender, oakmoss, angelica, clary sage, lime, fir, juniper, and bois de rose.

Tarragon pairs well with fennel and citrus and is wonderful with all kinds of fish. Its sharp flavor can provide punctuation to more homogeneous flavors, as in the poached chicken with tarragon recipe. It is strong, so use it sparingly as an accent. Tarragon should look bright green and vibrant. The tender leaves are very perishable, and left unrefrigerated for long, they'll wilt quickly.

IN THE EVERYDAY KITCHEN: Finish a quick sauté of mushrooms or vegetables with a drop or two of tarragon essential oil, or use it to flavor a sauce or vinaigrette. Add it to beurre blanc in place of rosewater (see page 117) to make a terrific sauce for fish.

The scent of tarragon—herbal, green, sweet, and licorice all at once—enlivens the spirits. Lime's sharp green burst adds lift, and the clary sage subtly deepens the blend. The synergy of these three essential oils creates an herbal scent that is rich and clean, and reminiscent of an afternoon spent puttering in an herb garden.

4 milliliters tarragon essential oil

3 milliliters clary sage essential oil

3 milliliters lime essential oil

Combine the essential oils in a small bottle, preferably one with a dropper cap. Add a dropperful to your diffuser or bath.

Tarragon-Marinated Beets with Frisée and Radishes

SERVES 8

For this salad, beets are roasted and then marinated with champagne vinegar, fruity olive oil, and tarragon essential oil, then served with a salad of frisée and radishes. The combination is a nice mix of flavors and textures. Be sure to cook the beets until they are fully tender to release all of their natural sweetness. The marinated beets on their own also make a nice side dish for grilled chicken or fish, and they keep well in the refrigerator for several days. If you can't find frisée, endive makes a good substitute.

3 pounds red beets, rinsed and top leaves trimmed

2 tablespoons pure olive oil

Salt and freshly ground black pepper

3 tablespoons champagne vinegar

1/3 cup plus 2 tablespoons fruity olive oil

10 drops tarragon essential oil

2 to 3 heads frisée, depending on size

1 bunch red radishes, trimmed and cut into eighths

1 tablespoon fresh lemon juice

Preheat the oven to 350°F. In a large mixing bowl, toss the beets with the pure olive oil, salt, and pepper. Put them in a heavy cast-iron skillet or roasting pan, add 1/4 cup water, and cover with aluminum foil. Place in the oven and cook until the beets are tender, about 1 1/2 to 2 hours, shaking the pan occasionally. Remove the beets to a plate to cool, then peel and cut them into 1/2-inch dice.

In a mixing bowl large enough to hold the cut beets, combine the champagne vinegar, ⅓ cup of fruity olive oil, and the essential oil. Add the beets to the bowl and toss, seasoning as necessary with salt and pepper. It may seem like a lot of liquid at first, but the beets will absorb most of it. Reserve the beets in their vinaigrette at room temperature, stirring occasionally, for 2 to 4 hours.

Trim the frisée by cutting off the dark green exterior leaves and cutting out the core at the bottom. Discard the dark green leaves, pull apart the blanched yellow interior leaves, rinse, and dry.

TO SERVE: Divide the beets among eight shallow soup bowls, spooning a little of the remaining vinaigrette around the beets. Toss the frisée and radishes with the lemon juice and the remaining 2 tablespoons of fruity olive oil, and season with salt and pepper. Mound the frisée and radish salad on top of the beets.

Seared Scallops with Tarragon Sabayon

SERVES 8

In this recipe, quickly seared sea scallops are paired with sweet spring vegetables and sauced with a frothy sabayon scented with tarragon. Although sabayon (a sauce made from egg yolks whisked over heat until light and foamy) is usually a dessert sauce, here it is made with vegetable stock and lemon juice. This delicate sauce also pairs well with salmon, halibut, and bass. The best scallops are "diver" or "day boat" scallops from Maine, which are harvested from November until April. They have an unmatched sweetness and texture, with the musky scent of the ocean. During the off-season, there are good scallops from Massachusetts and Canada—ask for "untreated" scallops for the best quality.

2 leeks, white and light green parts only, halved lengthwise, washed and sliced ¼ inch thick

2 tablespoons plus ½ cup fruity olive oil

Salt and freshly ground black pepper

¾ pound snap peas, trimmed and cut in half lengthwise

2 bunches large asparagus, peeled, halved lengthwise, and cut into 2-inch pieces

2 tablespoons pure olive oil

2½ pounds sea scallops

Tarragon Sabayon (page 78)

continued

Cook the leeks gently in the 2 tablespoons fruity olive oil with salt, covered, until tender. If it seems that the leeks are drying out, add a bit of water to keep them moist. When they are just tender, add ¼ cup of water and the remaining vegetables. Correct the salt and cook for 2 to 3 minutes more, until the peas and asparagus are tender. Remove from the heat and adjust the seasoning.

Prepare the Tarragon Sabayon.

TO SERVE: Heat the pure olive oil in a sauté pan to medium-high heat. Season the scallops with salt and black pepper and cook them for about 1 minute on both sides, until medium rare. Remove to a paper napkin–lined plate.

While the scallops are cooking, put a small pile of vegetables in the center of each plate, and spoon a generous amount of sabayon around the vegetables. Drizzle 1 tablespoon of the ½ cup fruity olive oil over each sabayon, then place the cooked scallops on top of the vegetables and around the plate. Serve immediately.

TARRAGON SABAYON

⅓ cup Vegetable Stock (page 197)

3 tablespoons fresh lemon juice

3 drops tarragon essential oil

2 large eggs

Salt

Whisk the ingredients together in a bowl, taste for seasoning, and pass through a fine mesh sieve. The salt is very important in this sauce, as it does not get corrected later, and without it, the sabayon will seem dull. The sauce can be prepared to this point and refrigerated for up to 2 days.

Place the tarragon-egg mixture in a heavy-bottomed 2-quart nonreactive pot over medium-low heat. Whisk vigorously, paying attention to the sides and corners of the pot. Move the pot from time to time so it does not develop hot spots. The sabayon will become light and fluffy and start to thicken. When you see the first few tiny bubbles beginning to pop through the surface of the sabayon (which should at this point be thick and somewhat mousselike), remove the pot from the heat, give it one or two stirs to get rid of any large bubbles, and set it on the side of the stove.

Poached Chicken with Tarragon

SERVES 8

In this updated classic French dish, the poaching liquid from the chicken is thickened with egg yolks to form a creamy sauce. This is a dish that both comforts, with its accompaniment of tender pearl onions and potatoes, and excites, with the tang of crème fraîche, the spiciness of Dijon mustard, and the intensity of tarragon.

16 creamer (new) potatoes

40 peeled pearl onions, preferably yellow

8 boneless chicken breasts, skin on

Salt and freshly ground black pepper

7 cups Chicken Stock (page 199)

4 large egg yolks

$1/3$ cup Crème Fraîche (page 200)

1 teaspoon Dijon mustard

1 teaspoon chopped fresh tarragon

5 drops tarragon essential oil

Cook the potatoes and the pearl onions in separate pots of well-salted water. Drain, cool, and reserve the onions. Drain, cool, peel, halve, and reserve the potatoes. Keep both the onions and the potatoes at room temperature.

Season the chicken breasts with salt and black pepper, cover, and let stand at room temperature for 20 minutes.

Heat 6 cups of the chicken stock to just below a simmer. Add the chicken and cook until it is firm to the touch and just cooked through, 10 to 15 minutes. Remove to a plate to rest for 2 minutes.

While the chicken is cooking, bring the remaining cup of chicken stock to a boil. Combine the egg yolks, crème fraîche, and mustard in a small mixing bowl. Whisk a few tablespoons of the hot chicken stock into the egg mixture and then pour that mixture back into the hot chicken stock. Reduce the heat and stir constantly until the sauce is thick enough to coat the back of a spoon. Stir in the chopped tarragon and tarragon essential oil, and adjust the seasoning with salt and black pepper. Add the reserved onions and potatoes to the sauce.

TO SERVE: Slice the chicken breasts and divide the slices among the eight soup dishes. Ladle some of the potatoes, onions, and sauce over the chicken breast and serve immediately.

PERILLA (SHISO)~

Perilla, which comes in green- and purple-leaved forms, is related to mint and basil. It is cultivated in Japan, China, Burma, and most recently, California. It has a unique herbal, floral, and exotic aroma. A *middle note* with relatively high intensity, it is useful in minute amounts, especially with florals such as ylang-ylang, jasmine, rose, and orange flower.

Buy fresh perilla by its Japanese name, *shiso*. The flavor of green shiso is kind of a cross between mint and cumin with spicy undertones, while red shiso has a more delicate roselike quality. Green shiso is available year-round, especially in the Asian markets, but red shiso is available only in the summer. Shiso is wonderful with all kinds of seafood and has an affinity for mint. The perilla essential oil is wonderful, perfectly capturing the essence of green shiso. When buying shiso, watch out for limp or dry-looking leaves, a sign of old age.

IN THE EVERYDAY KITCHEN: Try adding a few drops of perilla essential oil to lemon vinaigrette as an accompaniment to steamed fish. Brush grilled fish or chicken with Perilla-Infused Oil (page 82), or drizzle it on a carpaccio of raw fish.

ROSE AND PERILLA BOOKMARK

Leather is an excellent base for fragrance. A scented leather bookmark adds to the pleasure of reading. Scented leather sachets can also be used in your bureau or to scent letters kept in a stationery box.

In this fragrance, the perilla marries beautifully with the rose to make a scent that's mysterious yet light and cheerful.

20 drops rose absolute

4 drops perilla essential oil

**4-inch piece chamois cloth, washed
and air-dried**

Drop all the essences into a small bottle and shake to combine them. Leave them to marry for a week. Cut the chamois cloth into strips or whatever shape seems appealing as a bookmark or sachet. Drop the mixture onto chamois cloth. The scent will fade over time, so keep any excess oil to refresh the cloth later.

NOTE: Chamois is a soft, treated leather that is used to polish cars and can be purchased in automotive supply stores.

Turnip Soup with Perilla-Infused Oil

SERVES 8

Make this soup in winter when the turnips are sweetest. Their rich, spicy flavor, smoothed with a bit of butter, makes a lovely foil for the brightness of the shiso and mint. The trick is to cook the turnips until they are very, very soft to give the soup the most velvety texture. The soup can be made up to three days in advance. You will need to make the perilla oil the day before.

12 ounces peeled and sliced yellow onions (about 2 medium onions)

Salt

5 tablespoons unsalted butter

2½ pounds peeled and sliced turnips (8 to 10 turnips)

1 quart Vegetable Stock (page 197)

Freshly ground white pepper

Perilla-Infused Oil (recipe follows)

3 tablespoons chiffonade of fresh mint

FOR THE SOUP: In a nonreactive pot, cook the onions with some salt in 1 tablespoon of the butter, covered, over low heat until tender. Add the turnips, vegetable stock, and more salt, and cook until the turnips are very soft. Puree the soup in batches in a blender, adding a little of the remaining butter into each batch until it is all incorporated. Thin the soup with water if it seems too thick. Pass the soup through a strainer basket and season to taste with salt and white pepper.

TO SERVE: Divide the soup among eight bowls. Drizzle a generous teaspoon of perilla-infused oil over each soup and sprinkle with mint.

PERILLA-INFUSED OIL

¼ cup peanut oil

12 drops perilla essential oil

Combine the oils and let them stand in a sealed container for at least 24 hours before using.

Yellowtail Tartare with Shiso

SERVES 8

This is a fun and easy dish that uses radish, black sesame seeds, and shiso to highlight diced, raw yellowtail, called *hamachi* in Japanese. Because of the widespread popularity of sushi, it is now possible to get consistently high-quality farm-raised yellowtail from Japan year-round. Use three-inch ring molds to mold perfect circles of the tartare. It's no harder than it is to mound it on the plate, and the presentation is much sharper.

PERILLA VINAIGRETTE

Salt

1½ ounces rice wine vinegar

Perilla-Infused Oil (page 82)

YELLOWTAIL TARTARE

1½ teaspoons black sesame seeds

1 pound diced yellowtail

½ cup minced radish

Salt and freshly ground black pepper

2 tablespoons chiffonade of fresh shiso

FOR THE PERILLA VINAIGRETTE: In a mixing bowl, stir a few pinches of salt into the vinegar until it dissolves. Whisk in the perilla-infused oil and adjust the seasoning as necessary.

FOR THE TARTARE: Preheat the oven to 325°F. Spread the sesame seeds on a baking or sheet pan and bake, stirring occasionally, until the sesame seeds are aromatic, about 15 minutes. Cool.

Mix the yellowtail, radish, and sesame seeds in a mixing bowl. Add ⅔ of the perilla vinaigrette, salt, and black pepper and season to taste, adding more vinaigrette as necessary. You may end up with leftover vinaigrette; it can be kept in the refrigerator for up to 3 weeks.

TO SERVE: You can mound the tartare in small bowls, or use 3-inch-wide ring molds, creating a cylindrical shape by filling the molds with the tartare and gently pressing on the surface with a spoon to level it. Sprinkle some shiso over the top of the tartare and serve immediately (if it sits too long the acid in the vinaigrette will cause the fish to cook).

Heirloom Tomato and Yellow Doll Watermelon Salad

SERVES 8

Heirloom tomatoes are the flavorful varieties that were commonplace before tomatoes began to be grown for consistency and durability. They have names like Brandywine, Cherokee Purple, Marvel Stripe, Pineapple, Yellow Taxi, and Zebra, and they each have different flavors, colors, and sweet/tart balances. Get as many different kinds as you can find. You can also make this recipe with standard red tomatoes, but make sure they are ripe. Yellow Doll watermelon is yellow-fleshed, as the name implies, and is sweeter and more floral than regular watermelon, but regular watermelon will also work. Because peeling, seeding, and dicing the tomatoes is so messy, I do it in advance of preparing the dish so at the last minute I need only to combine the ingredients. Finally, if you cannot find red shiso, substitute green shiso, opal basil, or even regular basil.

12 to 15 medium-size heirloom tomatoes	⅓ cup chiffonade of fresh red shiso
2 cups diced Yellow Doll watermelon	¼ cup fruity green olive oil
1 teaspoon minced fresh ginger	Salt and freshly ground black pepper

FOR THE TOMATOES: Cut a small "x" in the bottoms of the tomatoes. Cook them in boiling water for about 10 seconds, and then remove to a plate to cool. Peel, seed, and dice the tomatoes into approximately ¼-inch pieces. Do not use the pieces close to the core that are tough and flavorless. Let the diced tomato sit in a piece of cheesecloth set into a strainer basket for 20 minutes to drain any excess liquid. This can be done several hours ahead. If you prepare the tomatoes in advance, keep them refrigerated until 20 minutes before assembling the rest of the salad.

FOR THE WATERMELON: Remove the rind and cut the watermelon into ¼-inch slices. Remove the seeds from the slices, cut the slices into strips, then cut the strips into cubes. Refrigerate the watermelon until serving.

TO SERVE: Toss the tomatoes and the watermelon with the ginger, shiso, and olive oil, and season with salt and black pepper. There should be three times as much diced tomato as watermelon, so you may want to measure the tomatoes first and then add the appropriate amount of watermelon. Divide the salad among eight bowls and serve immediately. Do not let it sit, or the salt will draw moisture out of the tomato and watermelon, creating kind of a soup rather than a salad.

LAVENDER ~

Lavender essential oil is distilled from the flowering tops of the lavender plant. Few people are unfamiliar with lavender's fresh, sweet fragrance, which starts out herbaceous, with a hint of eucalyptus, and becomes more flowery as it evolves. True lavender oil blends well with almost any other essence. Deep green lavender *absolute* and lavender *concrete* are more interesting, with a pronounced herbaceous scent that fades down to a woody, spicy pungency. They add a more full-bodied lavender odor to a perfume, blending well with labdanum, patchouli, vetiver, pine needle, and clary sage.

Because the actual plants contain such a high percentage of the strongly flavored essential oils, some recipes use only the plant. Lavender can be used in two forms, fresh or dried. The purple dried lavender from France is the best (see Sources, page 201). Lavender is a strong flavor that, like rosemary, is most effective when used in moderation—if used to excess, it can take on an unpleasant, soapy flavor. It pairs well with strongly flavored food like lamb and it can also lend distinction to sweet, understated ingredients, as in lavender-scented onions. When buying fresh lavender, try to find bunches of flowering lavender; its flavor is slightly sweeter and you can use the flowers as well. The lavender essential oil is extremely strong, so use it sparingly.

IN THE EVERYDAY KITCHEN: Pour a bottle of vodka over a bunch of fresh lavender, then refrigerate for one to two weeks, until the vodka is infused with the flavor and aroma of the lavender. Strain and use for martinis.

Lavender also combines beautifully with orange—try putting a drop of essential oil in an orange smoothie or orange custard. In fact, the Orange Flower Custard on page 109 would be equally wonderful if you use the lavender essential oil instead of neroli.

LAVENDER COLOGNE SPRAY

Lavender essential oil is such a familiar odor that this cologne, composed only of lavender, may come as a bit of a surprise. Lavender essential oil supplies the familiar camphorous, slightly medicinal lavender scent. Lavender absolute is more reminiscent of the flowering tops, somewhat sweet, rounded, and voluptuous. Lavender concrete renders the well-known lavender scent in a deep, earthy, soft version. This beautiful turquoise-hued cologne is not overly flowery and can be worn by either sex.

¼ teaspoon lavender concrete

30 milliliters grape alcohol

30 drops lavender absolute

40 drops lavender essential oil

Add the lavender concrete to the alcohol and stir to dissolve. Add the drops of absolute and essential oil. Shake and let sit for a week. Before using, strain the mixture through a plastic coffee filter fitted with unbleached paper. The solids from the lavender concrete will be caught by the paper, and the resulting cologne will be a clear and bright aquamarine.

Grilled Steak with Onion-Potato Compote Scented with Lavender

SERVES 8

This compote is a simple, yet satisfying side dish for a steak. Where traditionally the onions and potatoes might be fried crisp, here they create a soft, moist mixture perfumed with the floral yet masculine scent of lavender. The dish is drizzled with balsamic vinegar, which brightens the combination, and the flavor of the balsamic pairs wonderfully with the lavender. For the balsamic vinegar, use the best you can find. If you use a *tradizionale* vinegar, the best and rarest balsamic made (see Sources, page 201), increase the amount, as it is relatively low in acidity. You can make the compote the day before.

Salt and freshly ground black pepper

16 creamer (new) potatoes, preferably yellow Finn or Yukon gold

1 tablespoon unsalted butter

4 medium yellow onions, peeled and thinly sliced

2 to 3 teaspoons minced fresh lavender

8 steaks

3 tablespoons excellent-quality balsamic vinegar

Cook the potatoes in well-salted water until tender. Remove to a plate to cool. In a nonreactive pot, melt the butter over medium-low heat and add the sliced onions and some salt. Cook, covered, stirring occasionally, until the onions are meltingly tender. While the onions are cooking, peel the potatoes and cut them into small pieces, either quarters or sixths depending on their size. Add the cut potatoes to the onions and cook for 2 minutes more, stirring to combine. Remove from the heat and stir in 2 teaspoons of the lavender, adding more if needed. Season with salt if necessary. Hold warm while you cook the steaks, or if you make the compote in advance, cool it down by spreading it out on a plate and refrigerating until needed.

Season the steaks with salt and pepper and grill them. (Sauté them in pure olive oil if you are cooking indoors.) Let them rest a few minutes, and serve with the onion-potato compote next to them. Drizzle the balsamic vinegar around the steak and compote.

Lavender Roasted Chicken

In this simple recipe, chicken and vegetables are slowly roasted and perfumed with fresh lavender. The low oven temperature keeps the meat moist and tender and allows the vegetables to absorb the juices of the chicken as they cook. For variations on the basic recipe, you can replace the lavender with rosemary, sage, or thyme. The recipe can be doubled for a larger group, but you will need either a roasting pan large enough to comfortable hold two chickens plus vegetables, or two roasting pans.

1 whole chicken (about 3½ to 4 pounds)

Salt and freshly ground black pepper

1 small bunch fresh lavender

2 tablespoons unsalted butter

1 large carrot, peeled and sliced ½ inch thick

1 medium yellow onion, peeled, halved and sliced ½ inch thick

1 leek, white and light green parts only, halved lengthwise, rinsed and sliced ½ inch thick

1 fennel bulb, halved lengthwise, cored, and sliced ½ inch thick

1 tablespoon fruity olive oil

Preheat the oven to 325°F. Rinse the chicken inside and out under cold water and pat dry. Season generously inside and out with salt and pepper and let stand at room temperature, loosely covered, for 20 minutes.

Pick off and mince 1 teaspoon of lavender leaves. Stuff the cavity of the chicken with the remaining lavender and the butter. Place in the center of a roasting pan breast side down. Toss the vegetables in a mixing bowl with the olive oil, minced lavender, salt, and pepper. Scatter them in the roasting pan around the chicken and put the pan in the oven.

Stir the vegetables every 10 minutes, and after 30 minutes turn the chicken on its back. Roast for 40 to 50 minutes more, occasionally stirring the vegetables and basting the chicken with any liquid that accumulates in the roasting pan, until the juices of the chicken run clear when the leg is pierced with a knife. Remove the pan from the oven and let stand at room temperature for 20 minutes. Taste the vegetables and season as necessary with salt and pepper.

Carve the chicken and serve it with the vegetables, spooning some of the juices from the roasting pan over each serving.

Lavender Shortbread Cookies

MAKES ABOUT 40 TO 50 COOKIES, pictured on page 67

This dough makes for wonderfully addictive cookies that scent the entire house as they bake. As with all dough, the key is making sure that the dough is well combined but not overworked, which makes it tough. Although some shortbread cookies are rolled extremely thick, this can lead to doughy cookies that are not cooked all the way through. Roll the cookies a bit thinner so that they will cook evenly. Any leftover dough can be stored in the freezer, well wrapped, for two months.

4 ounces sugar (1/2 cup plus 1 tablespoon), plus more for sprinkling

12 drops lavender essential oil

1/8 teaspoon salt

8 ounces (2 sticks) unsalted butter

1 large egg

12 ounces (2 1/3 cups) cake flour

1 large egg white

1 1/2 tablespoons dried lavender flowers

In a food processor, blend the sugar and essential oil for 15 seconds, until well combined. Add the salt and the butter, then pulse until the butter is well incorporated. Add the egg and pulse until incorporated. Add the flour and carefully pulse, until the dough forms small pebblelike shapes. Remove the dough from the food processor and gently combine by hand until smooth. Wrap and refrigerate for at least 2 hours.

Roll out the dough to a thickness of 5 millimeters (about 1/4 inch). Cut the dough into whatever shapes you prefer, transfer to a baking sheet lined with parchment, and refrigerate for about 20 minutes.

Preheat the oven to 325°F. Whisk the egg white in a mixing bowl for about 10 seconds, until it is somewhat frothy and well combined. Remove the cookies from the refrigerator, brush with egg white, and sprinkle with sugar and the lavender flowers. Bake until the edges are just starting to turn golden brown, about 10 to 15 minutes. Let them cool and serve. Resist the temptation to serve them warm from the oven, as their flavor and texture will improve when they have cooled.

Floral

Litsea Cubeba
Chamomile
Orange Flower
Jasmine
Rose

CLOCKWISE FROM TOP LEFT: Mint, Basil, and Coriander Bath Salts (page 39); epsom salts; Saffron, Ginger, and Blood Orange Bath Salts (page 192); cocoa perfume; ylang-ylang essential oil; benzoin resin; lavender absolute; saffron absolute; ginger essential oil. OPPOSITE, FROM TOP LEFT: rosemary sprig, rose, jasmine pearls, vanilla bean, orange with its leaves and flowers.

LITSEA CUBEBA~

Litsea cubeba, distilled from the fruit of the may chang tree, a Chinese member of the laurel family, has a fresh, sweet, and intense lemony fragrance. It blends well with all citrus oils, as well as with petitgrain, rosemary, and lavender. Unlike lemon oil, litsea cubeba never goes rancid. Because of its floral citrus aroma, litsea is useful as a substitute for lemon verbena, which is very expensive and often adulterated.

Litsea cubeba is a showstopper when used in cooking. Its intense aroma and flavor has similarities to both lemongrass and lemon verbena, but with an explosiveness that is all its own. It goes best with brightly flavored dishes and ingredients, and pairs well with saffron, artichokes, tomatoes, and seafood, as well as tropical fruits. It is powerful and should be used carefully because it will be the dominant note in whatever dish it is in; therefore the other aromatic components should be supporting it, not competing.

IN THE EVERYDAY KITCHEN: A few drops of litsea cubeba essential oil can transform a traditional crab or lobster salad. Mixed with citrus vinaigrette, it adds a pleasing floral note. Drizzle the Litsea Cubeba–Infused Oil (page 97) over a sauté or soup of spring vegetables.

Litsea cubeba has such great odor intensity that the small amount used in this recipe holds its own against the other scents. Both the cedarwood and the nutmeg lend a clean, light woodiness to the blend. Rooibas, a lovely amber-colored herb that is used to make tea, adds a sweet, berrylike note.

1 milliliter litsea cubeba essential oil	1 milliliter rooibas absolute
2 milliliters Virginia cedarwood essential oil	2 milliliters nutmeg essential oil

Combine the essences in a small bottle, preferably one with a dropper cap. Add a dropperful to your diffuser or bath.

Steamed Artichokes with Litsea Cubeba Mayonnaise

SERVES 8

In this easy and delicious appetizer, large artichokes are steamed until tender and served with mayonnaise flavored with litsea cubeba. The mayonnaise gets brightness from lemon juice, and the fragrant litsea cubeba adds a floral note. Although artichokes are available year-round, the best time to buy them is in the spring and fall, when their quality is at its best.

8 large artichokes	50 drops litsea cubeba essential oil
2 large egg yolks	Salt and freshly ground black pepper
2 tablespoons fresh lemon juice	2$\frac{1}{2}$ cups pure olive oil

Stand the artichokes upright in a steamer basket set over simmering water. Cook until the artichokes are tender, about 45 minutes to 1 hour.

While the artichokes are cooking make the mayonnaise. In a mixing bowl, whisk the egg yolks, lemon juice, essential oil, and salt until well combined. Drizzle in the olive oil a few drops at a time until it forms an emulsion, at which time you can increase the flow of oil to a slow, steady stream. When all the oil is added, adjust the seasoning with salt and pepper as necessary. Divide among eight small bowls.

When the artichokes are tender, remove them from the heat and cool slightly. Serve them on plates, with a bowl of mayonnaise for dipping the meaty ends of the leaves, and another bowl for discarding the tough ends of the leaves.

Black Bass with Litsea Cubeba and Saffron-Citrus Sauce

SERVES 8

Black bass, an ocean fish caught off the coast of Rhode Island, has an intense sweetness and elegant texture. Ask for it scaled and filleted, but with the skin on, as it has a pleasant flavor and texture and protects the fish while it cooks. It is served here on a bed of braised lettuce and fennel with a saffron-citrus sauce drizzled with litsea cubeba–infused olive oil. The lettuce and fennel create a refreshing complement for the full flavor of the fish, and the combined aroma of the saffron-citrus sauce and the litsea cubeba is exhilarating. You can substitute any sweet white-fleshed fish, such as halibut or snapper, for the black bass.

Saffron-Citrus Sauce (recipe follows)

Salt and freshly ground black pepper

4 hearts of romaine

2 fennel bulbs, cut into julienne strips

1 tablespoon pure olive oil

Eight 5-ounce pieces black bass fillet, skins on but bones removed (your fishmonger can do this for you)

Litsea Cubeba–Infused Oil (recipe follows)

Make the saffron-citrus sauce and hold it warm.

Bring a pot of well-salted water to a boil. Cook the hearts of romaine for 2 to 3 minutes, or until crisp-tender and bright green. Lift out the lettuce, reserving the cooking water, put the lettuce in a bowl, and cover with ice. After 3 minutes, squeeze all of the water out of the romaine, chop the cooked romaine into bite-size pieces, and transfer to a saucepan. Bring the cooking water from the romaine back to a boil and cook the fennel until tender, about 4 to 5 minutes. Drain the fennel and add it to the pot containing the romaine. Add the saffron-citrus sauce to the vegetables and warm gently over low heat.

Heat the pure olive oil in a sauté pan to medium-high. Season the fish with salt on both sides and with black pepper on the flesh side only. Sauté the bass skin side down for about 3 minutes, then turn the pieces over and cook for only a few seconds more. Transfer the fish to a plate lined with a paper towel to drain.

TO SERVE: While the fish is cooking, divide the vegetables among eight soup plates, mounding them in the center of each plate, and pouring some sauce around the vegetables. Drizzle about 1½ teaspoons of the litsea cubeba oil on top of the sauce. Place the fish on top of the vegetables and serve immediately.

SAFFRON-CITRUS SAUCE

½ cup dry white wine

1 cup Chicken Stock (page 199)

½ teaspoon saffron threads

3 ounces fresh orange juice

1 tablespoon fresh lime juice

1 teaspoon champagne vinegar

12 tablespoons unsalted butter, cut into small pieces

Salt

Bring the white wine to a boil, cook for 1 minute and add the chicken stock and saffron. Remove from the heat and let stand for 10 minutes.

Add the orange juice, lime juice, and champagne vinegar, and put the pot back on the stove over low-medium heat. When the liquid is warm, whisk in the butter a few pieces at a time until the butter is completely incorporated. Season with salt and pass the sauce through a fine mesh sieve.

LITSEA CUBEBA–INFUSED OIL

25 drops litsea cubeba essential oil

¼ cup pure olive oil

Mix the two oils together, preferably 1 to 2 days in advance so that they can marry.

Pineapple–Litsea Cubeba Granita

SERVES 6 TO 8

The litsea cubeba in this simple granita accents the floral aroma of pineapple. As pineapples vary quite a bit in sweetness, you'll need to sweeten to taste. Well covered, you can keep the granita frozen for a week or so, but an extended period in the freezer will dull the flavor.

1 pineapple, as ripe as possible	1 to 2 cups Simple Syrup (page 200)
1 tablespoon fresh lemon juice	6 to 8 drops litsea cubeba essential oil

Cut the skin off the pineapple (core if necessary) and cut the meat into 1-inch cubes. Put the pineapple in a blender with the lemon juice and ¾ cup of the simple syrup. Blend for 45 seconds, until completely smooth. Pass the mixture through a fine mesh sieve and season to taste with litsea cubeba essential oil and more of the simple syrup as needed. Keep in mind that the granita will lose a little sweetness when frozen, so sweeten more than you think you should. Pour the mixture into a wide, shallow container (which will make it easier to scrape) and freeze solid. Cover if you do not plan to serve it that night. To serve, scrape the ice vigorously with a fork until you form a mound of granita. Scoop into chilled bowl. You can scrape the granita in advance, if you like, and leave it in a sealed container in the freezer for up to 4 hours.

CHAMOMILE~

Chamomile, one of the most popular scents in aromatherapy, is calming and relaxing. This sweet, fruity, applelike *top note* grows warmer and more herbal as it fades. Chamomile lends a freshness and natural depth to a fragrance, blending well with bergamot, oakmoss, labdanum, neroli, and clary sage. If too enthusiastically dosed, however, it will overpower other essences in a blend.

For cooking purposes, on the other hand, dried chamomile flowers tend to be meek and must be used in exaggerated amounts. The tea provides a more versatile base for cooking with than the essential oil, although the essential oil can be helpful in reinforcing the flavor. You don't need to use a particular brand of chamomile, as long as the flavor is true. Chamomile loves sweet and subtle accompaniments, and lemon enlivens its flavor without changing its nature.

IN THE EVERYDAY KITCHEN: For a wonderfully fragrant accompaniment to fish or chicken, try making a pot of chamomile tea, straining out the leaves, then cooking white rice in the resulting liquid.

CHAMOMILE AND YLANG-YLANG FACE ELIXIR

Face elixirs are nothing like commercial night creams—more like a treat than a treatment. On a clean face before bed, the elixir melts into the skin in about 20 minutes, leaving no oily residue. You drift off to sleep amid beautiful aromas and wake up to skin that feels soft and smells beautiful.

This particular elixir is best for normal or sensitive skin. The bright apple fragrance of the chamomile combines with the sweetness of the ylang-ylang to create an easy, fruity fragrance, comforting to mind and body. Chamomile is soothing, and ylang-ylang helps regulate the skin. The base oils of apricot kernel, squalene, and rose hip seed oils are emollient and rejuvenating and easily absorbed into the skin.

10 milliliters apricot kernel oil

2¹/₂ milliliters squalene

2¹/₂ milliliters rose hip seed oil

6 drops chamomile essential oil

4 drops ylang-ylang extra essential oil

Combine the apricot kernel oil with the squalene and rose hip seed oil. Stir with a stirring stick to mix. Add the drops of essences. Store in a small bottle and keep for up to 4 months. Shake before using.

Chamomile-Scented Veal Tenderloin

SERVES 8

Perfect for a light meal, this is a dish of subtle but comforting flavors and aromas. The veal is poached in a "stock" made from chamomile tea and essential oil, and that poaching liquid is then used to scent an accompanying mixture of julienned zucchini and leeks. When cutting the zucchini, it helps to use a mandoline with the medium cutter attachments, but if you are cutting by hand, just get them as fine and even as possible.

CHAMOMILE STOCK

8 cups very hot water

7 bags chamomile tea

3 drops chamomile essential oil

3 medium leeks, white and light green parts only

3 yellow zucchini

3 green zucchini

Two 1¼-pound pieces veal tenderloin, trimmed of silvery skin and connective tissue

Salt and freshly ground black pepper

2 teaspoons fresh lemon zest

3 tablespoons fruity olive oil

FOR THE CHAMOMILE STOCK: Pour the water over the chamomile bags and let steep for 5 to 8 minutes, until the flavor is very strong but not bitter. Remove the tea bags, squeezing out any water left in the bags as you remove them. Stir in the essential oil.

FOR THE LEEKS: Remove the tough outside layer of the leeks, cut them into 2-inch segments, and then cut each segment in half lengthwise. Peel two or three layers off the leeks at a time, flatten them stacked one on top of the other, and cut them into fine julienne strips.

FOR THE ZUCCHINI: Trim the ends, cut them into 2-inch segments, and finely julienne them using the medium blade of the mandoline, or by hand. Discard the seedy pulp and save it for another use, such as soup.

FOR THE VEAL: Season the veal pieces with salt and black pepper and let them stand at room temperature, covered, for 20 minutes. Bring the chamomile stock up to about 150°F, just below simmering, and add the veal to the pot. Cook over low heat until the veal is medium rare, about 10 to 14 minutes, then remove the veal to a plate to rest. While the veal is poaching, cook the leeks gently in a covered container with salt in 1 tablespoon of the olive oil until tender. After removing the veal from the stock, add the zucchini to the pot with the leeks, along with 1 cup of the chamomile stock and some salt. Cook over medium heat, stirring often, until the zucchini is tender, about 2 minutes.

Remove from the heat, add the lemon zest and the remaining 2 tablespoons olive oil, and season with salt and black pepper.

TO SERVE: Slice the veal and arrange on warm plates, and then put a pile of the zucchini–leek mixture next to the veal. Sprinkle some salt on the veal, add a little bit of the cooking liquid from the vegetables, and serve immediately.

Steamed Halibut
with Lemon-Chamomile Sauce

SERVES 8

In this dish, a classic lemon-butter sauce is scented with chamomile. The halibut is steamed and set on top of braised endives, whose delicate crunch and refreshing bitterness plays well against the fragrant chamomile and the sweet halibut. The vegetable stock that replaces the traditional chicken or fish stock makes for a lighter dish and a better conduit for flavor. Make sure that the endives are cooked through; otherwise they will tend to discolor and the texture will not be as refined.

BRAISED ENDIVES

3 cups Vegetable Stock (page 197)

1/3 cup dry white wine

1/4 cup fresh lemon juice

2 tablespoons sugar

Salt

8 whole endives

Lemon-Chamomile Sauce (recipe follows)

Eight 5-ounce pieces of halibut

Salt and freshly ground black pepper

2 tablespoons pure olive oil

FOR THE BRAISED ENDIVES: In a nonreactive pot, bring the vegetable stock, wine, lemon juice, sugar, and some salt to a gentle simmer. Add the endives and cook, covered, until tender. The endives will stay a bit whiter if you cover them with a piece of parchment or a few layers of cheesecloth, but this is not crucial. When the endives are done, remove them to a plate to cool. Trim the root ends, which tend to discolor, and cut each endive in half lengthwise.

While the endives are cooking, make the Lemon-Chamomile Sauce and keep it warm in a water bath (see page 34).

FOR THE FISH: Season the halibut with salt on both sides and black pepper on the bottom only. Place in a steamer basket over simmering water until just cooked through, 4 to 8 minutes.

While the fish is cooking, heat the olive oil to medium-high in a sauté pan. Place the endives in the pan flat sides down and cook until nicely browned; turn and brown the other side. Remove to a plate and sprinkle with salt.

TO SERVE: Place 2 pieces of endive in the center of warm plates or wide shallow bowls. When the fish is cooked, place it on top of the endive, and pour about an ounce of sauce over and around the fish.

LEMON-CHAMOMILE SAUCE	6 tablespoons unsalted butter, cut into ½-ounce pieces
5 bags chamomile tea	
1 cup very hot water	1 tablespoon fresh lemon juice
	Salt

Cut the tops off of the tea bags and empty the chamomile into a pot. Add the hot water and let it stand off of the heat for 5 minutes. Put the pot on a low flame and begin whisking in the butter, a few pieces at a time, until it is all incorporated. Remove from the heat, and add the lemon juice and season with salt to taste. Pass the sauce through a fine mesh sieve, pressing firmly on the solids to extract all of the liquid, and hold warm. This should not be done too far in advance, at most an hour before.

Chamomile and Almond Soufflé Cake

SERVES 6 TO 8

This may be the perfect afternoon tea cake—moist, nutty, and infused with the flavor and aroma of chamomile tea.

¼ cup sliced almonds

2 ounces unsalted butter, melted, plus additional for buttering pan

Flour, for flouring pan

8 bags chamomile tea

6 ounces whole blanched almonds

6 ounces sugar (¾ cup), plus more for serving plate

Salt

4 large eggs, 1 separated

Zest of 1 lemon, finely chopped

1 ounce (3 tablespoons) cornstarch

¼ teaspoon baking powder

Confectioners' sugar, for dusting

Preheat the oven to 300°F. Toast the sliced almonds for 15 minutes, stirring occasionally. Cool. Butter and flour a 9-inch cake pan. Sprinkle the toasted almonds on the bottom of the pan. Turn up the oven to 320°F.

Remove the chamomile tea from the bags. In a food processor, process the whole blanched almonds, sugar, a pinch of salt, and chamomile into a paste. This will take several minutes. If the mixture is dry, add 1 egg white to form a paste. Otherwise, add the white at the very end of the processing and combine.

Transfer the almond paste to a mixer fitted with the paddle attachment. Add 1 yolk and 1 egg and beat on low for 1 minute. Add another egg and beat for another minute. Add the last egg and the lemon zest and beat for about 5 more minutes, or until the mixture is light in color and increased in volume.

With a rubber spatula, fold in the cornstarch and baking powder until mostly combined. Use as few strokes as possible. Add the melted butter and fold in until just combined. If you overmix the batter, it will knock out the incorporated air.

Pour the batter a little more than halfway up the sides of the prepared cake pan. Bake at 320°F for about 40 minutes, or until the top is just set. Because the cake is so tender, it will feel soft to the touch even when fully cooked.

Remove the cake from the oven and let it stand for 3 minutes. Sprinkle a plate generously with sugar and then turn the cake out onto the plate (because the cake is flourless, without the sugar it will stick to the plate). Cool fully, then cover until ready to serve. Dust with the confectioners' sugar, slice, and serve.

ORANGE FLOWER ~

When orange flowers from the bitter orange tree are distilled, they yield neroli essential oil and orange flower hydrosol. Cool, elegant, and floral, orange flower water adds a sophisticated note to any blend.

Orange flower water is a *hydrosol,* a by-product of the essential oil–making process. It has a powerfully seductive fragrance and flavor, heady with the essence of orange blossoms. Use it sparingly with lean food, and a bit more generously with fat-laden food, as it is fat soluble and will need to have its flavor reinforced in the company of butter or cream. Orange flower water is usually available in Middle Eastern food stores. Neroli essential oil is a revelation—orange flowers magnified. A few drops transform a classic custard dish as in the orange flower custard recipe, but it can also be used for flavoring ice cream or giving a different dimension to orange sorbet.

IN THE EVERYDAY KITCHEN: For a beautifully perfumed sorbet, try adding a few drops of neroli essential oil. Try mixing orange flower water with honey and drizzling it over yogurt. A splash mixed in with apples before baking makes a delightfully fragrant addition to apple pie.

These three hydrosols blended together create a rich floral aroma. Orange flower hydrosol has an ambrosial floral scent with almost masculine undertones. The rose and sandalwood hydrosols soften its rough edges. This is a wonderful mixture on your pillowcase before bed, or to spray on your face to both moisturize your skin and make it fragrant.

10 milliliters rose hydrosol

5 milliliters orange flower hydrosol

10 milliliters sandalwood hydrosol

Pour all three hydrosols into a spray bottle and keep refrigerated. It is best used within 4 months.

Winter Vegetable Curry Accented with Orange Flower Water

SERVES 8

This is a warming winter vegetable stew that combines the heat of curry with the sultry fragrance of orange flower water. It is essentially a one-pot endeavor, which makes it even more appealing. First the vegetables are slowly cooked with curry, and then half of the vegetables are removed and the remaining vegetables are cooked in vegetable stock until soft, then pureed. The resulting liquid is something in between a stock and a sauce. How thick it becomes is up to you. Orange flower water is fat soluble, so it takes quite a bit to saturate the sauce before its flavor and aroma are evident. Keep the orange flower water handy when finishing the dish, as it may need a splash more just before serving. This dish can be made a day or two in advance, but then the orange flower aroma will fade and will probably need to be refreshed when reheating.

VEGETABLES

10 ounces celery root
(1 to 2 celery roots)

10 ounces parsnip (about 2 parsnips)

10 ounces fennel (1 to 2 bulbs)

6 ounces leek, white and light green
parts only (about 3 leeks)

9 ounces carrots (about 3 carrots)

1 tablespoon unsalted butter

1 tablespoon plus 1 teaspoon
Madras curry

Salt

SAUCE

3 cups Vegetable Stock (page 197)

5½ ounces peeled and sliced sweet
apple, such as Fuji

2 tablespoons unsalted butter

2 tablespoons orange flower water

1 tablespoon fresh lime juice

Salt

FOR THE VEGETABLES: Peel and cut all the vegetables into even ¼-inch-thick slices.

Melt the butter over low heat in a heavy-bottomed pot with a lid. Add the vegetables, curry, and salt and cook, covered, stirring often, until the vegetables are tender, about 30 minutes. Add salt as necessary and remove all but 3 cups of vegetables to a separate pot and hold warm, or if you are making the recipe in advance, cool and refrigerate until needed.

FOR THE SAUCE: Add the vegetable stock and the apple to the 3 cups of vegetables in the original cooking pot and simmer until the vegetables are very tender, about 30 to 45 minutes. Puree the vegetables and liquid in a blender in batches with the butter. Thin with water as necessary to achieve the desired consistency (keep in mind that you can always thin the sauce more when you serve the stew, but you can never rethicken it, so thin with caution).

Add the orange flower water and the lime juice and season with salt as needed. If you are making the recipe in advance, cool and reserve.

TO SERVE: Heat the vegetables and the sauce together until hot. Season with more orange flower water, lime juice, or salt if necessary, and ladle into soup bowls.

Dried Fruits Marinated in Orange Flower Water

SERVES 6 TO 8

In this dish, orange flower water is added to a mixture of marinated dried fruits. The tapioca is flavored with sweet orange, which adds another dimension to the exotic perfume of orange flower blossoms.

Use the best-quality dried fruits you can find, and feel free to add or subtract fruits according to their quality and availability. The dried fruits are listed by both volume and weight. Some of the steps, like soaking the tapioca and marinating the dried fruit, need to be done the day before.

MARINATED DRIED FRUITS

3 ounces (²/₃ cup) dried apricots

2 ounces (¹/₂ cup) dried pears

1¹/₂ ounces (¹/₃ cup) dried figs

1¹/₂ ounces (¹/₃ cup) golden raisins

1¹/₂ ounces (¹/₃ cup) dried apples

1 ounce (¹/₄ cup) dried currants

1 cup water

¹/₄ cup fresh orange juice

¹/₄ cup sugar

1 tablespoon orange flower water

1¹/₂ teaspoons fresh lemon juice

TAPIOCA

Heaping ¹/₃ cup (2 ounces) small tapioca pearls

1 cup fresh orange juice

1 cup water

Grated zest of 1 orange

¹/₄ cup plus 1 tablespoon sugar

1 tablespoon fresh lemon juice

FOR THE MARINATED FRUITS: Dice the dried fruits into ¹/₃-inch pieces and place them in a bowl. Bring the water, orange juice, and sugar to a boil. Off the heat, add the orange flower water and the lemon juice, then pour the liquid over the dried fruits. Let them cool at room temperature, stirring occasionally. When fully cooled, refrigerate. This can be done the same day, but the dried fruit is best when it has 1 or 2 days to macerate.

FOR THE TAPIOCA: The night before, cover the tapioca pearls in cold water and refrigerate. The next day, bring the orange juice, water, orange zest, and sugar to a simmer. Drain the tapioca pearls through a strainer and then lower the strainer with the tapioca into the boiling liquid, tilting the strainer to release the tapioca. Stir carefully to make sure that the tapioca does not stick to the bottom of the pot. Gently simmer the tapioca, stirring occasionally, until the pearls are translucent and tender, 3 to 5 minutes.

Add the lemon juice, taste to see if you need more lemon juice or sugar, then pour the tapioca into a container and refrigerate.

TO SERVE: Spoon some tapioca into bowls and top with the dried fruits and a little bit of syrup from the marinade.

Orange Flower Custard

SERVES 8

Neroli, orange flower essential oil, has a flavor and aroma that is far more exciting than orange flower water, although its uses are more limited. Here the fragrant neroli, juxtaposed with the familiarity of the cool, creamy custard, makes an exciting combination. The custards will set up considerably as they cool, so be careful not to overcook them. Keeping the oven temperature low will help give you a longer window in which they are properly cooked. For this recipe, you will need eight 4-ounce heatproof ceramic cups or ramekins.

5 large eggs	2 cups heavy cream
2 large egg yolks	1 cup fresh orange juice
½ cup sugar	8 drops neroli essential oil
1 cup whole milk	Salt

Preheat the oven to 275°F. In a mixing bowl, whisk the eggs and yolks with the sugar until just combined. Bring the milk and cream to just below a boil, cool slightly, and then whisk into the eggs. Add the orange juice, neroli oil, and a pinch of salt. Strain the mixture through a fine mesh sieve, and skim any foam that may float to the top.

Pour equal amounts of the custard mixture into eight heatproof ceramic cups. Place the cups in a large roasting pan, transfer the pan to the oven, and then, using a pitcher, fill the pan with hot water to about halfway up the sides of the cups. Cover the top of the pan with aluminum foil. Bake for 30 to 45 minutes (or more, depending on the size and shape of your cups), or until the custards are set around the edges but jiggle slightly in the center when lightly shaken. They will continue to set as they cool down, so they should be a bit loose. Remove the foil and cool at room temperature for 10 minutes, then refrigerate until chilled, at least 4 hours.

They will keep at least 2 days in the refrigerator, but they are best the day they are made. Serve them straight from the refrigerator in their baking ramekins.

JASMINE ~

Jasmine is probably the most important perfume material. Rich, warm, heavy, and intensely floral, it has the ability to seize the senses and the imagination. Its sweetness gives way to a drier note as it evolves, and it retains its warmth and depth as it fades. More than two thousand pounds of flowers produce a little less than two pounds of jasmine *absolute*. Jasmine *concrete* is a solid, reddish-orange wax whose sweet, mellow tone lends smoothness to any blend. Powerful as it is, jasmine refreshes rather than oppresses, possessing both antidepressant and aphrodisiacal properties.

As incomparable as its aroma is, jasmine is of limited use in cooking. The absolute has an almost overwhelming animalistic flavor that makes it difficult to integrate into a dish, so the recipes all use infusions made with jasmine pearls (see Sources, page 201), which is a kind of jasmine tea. Jasmine pearls work best with ingredients that share its sweet, ethereal nature and where the jasmine can provide a distinct note without being overwhelming.

IN THE EVERYDAY KITCHEN: Brew a pot of jasmine tea until strong but not bitter, and freeze in ice cube trays. Blend the cubes with peaches, yogurt, and a pinch of sugar to make delicious smoothies. Use the Jasmine Syrup (page 111) to marinate fresh fruit, or to add a haunting note to sorbet.

JASMINE LIQUID PERFUME

Combining two species of one plant adds depth to a floral aroma. Here the spiciness of the jasmine sambac balances out the voluptuousness of grandiflorum jasmine in the concrete and absolute. All the other ingredients have been chosen for their ability to enhance this heavy and intense wintry perfume.

6 drops Peru balsam resin

12 drops fir absolute

9 drops labdanum absolute

1/8 teaspoons grandiflorum jasmine concrete

5 drops jasmine sambac absolute

4 drops grandiflorum jasmine absolute

5 drops coriander essential oil

10 drops sweet orange essential oil

15 milliliters ethyl alcohol

Drop the essences into the alcohol and stir with a stirring stick. Pour into a bottle and let marry for a week or more. Before using, strain the mixture through a plastic coffee filter lined with unbleached paper. Decant into an appealing small bottle, preferably one with a ground glass stopper. This beautiful amber-colored perfume will age over time, growing deeper and smoother.

White Peach–Jasmine Sorbet

SERVES 8

The floral notes of the white peaches and jasmine work in concert as if they were made for each other. The sweetness and jasmine flavor in the base should seem a bit strong, as the freezing process dulls both flavor and aroma. You can serve the sorbet by itself or on a bed of white peaches tossed with some sugar.

3 pounds ripe white peaches, peeled and sliced (about 12 peaches)

1/4 cup fresh lemon juice

Jasmine Syrup (recipe follows)

In a blender, puree all of the ingredients together. Add more lemon juice or sugar if necessary. Keep in mind that the sorbet will taste a little less sweet once it is frozen. Pass the mixture through a fine mesh sieve and freeze in your sorbet machine according to the manufacturer's directions.

JASMINE SYRUP

1 cup sugar

3 cups water

2 tablespoons jasmine pearls

Dissolve the sugar in the water and heat to a boil. Add the jasmine pearls and remove from the heat. Let stand for 10 minutes and then strain through a fine mesh sieve.

Jasmine-Steamed Chicken Breast

SERVES 8, pictured on page 66

The jasmine in this recipe adds an otherworldly note to a springtime medley of sweet peas, carrots, onions, and lettuce. By making what is essentially a jasmine stock (in other circumstances it would be thought of as a strong pot of tea), cooking the vegetables in that stock, and then using a minimal amount of fat, the jasmine aromas can blossom without taking over. The chicken comes to the table with the whisper of jasmine all around it, but the chicken flavor remains the focus of the dish. If you omit the chicken, the vegetables and broth make a simple appetizer or side dish. Spring onions, onions that have not yet formed a papery skin, have a sweet mild flavor. If they are not available, you can substitute yellow onions.

8 boneless chicken breasts, skin on

Salt and freshly ground black pepper

4 spring onions or 2 medium yellow onions, peeled and thinly sliced (about 14 ounces unpeeled)

1 tablespoon pure olive oil

2 carrots, halved lengthwise and sliced ¼ inch thick (about 2 cups)

2 cups water

1 tablespoon jasmine pearls

2 hearts of romaine, chopped into ½-inch pieces

2 cups shelled peas (about 1¾ pounds unshelled)

Season the chicken with salt and black pepper and let stand at room temperature for 20 minutes. Bring some water to a simmer in the bottom of a steamer. Place the breasts in a steamer basket and steam until they are just cooked through, about 15 minutes. Remove the chicken to a plate to rest.

After you salt the chicken, you can begin preparing the rest of the dish.

Cook the onions gently in a heavy pot with the olive oil and salt, covered, until tender. Uncover and remove from the heat.

While the onions are cooking, boil the carrots in salted water until tender. Drain and spread on a plate to cool. For the jasmine infusion, bring the water to just below a boil and pour into a bowl containing the jasmine pearls. Let stand for 8 minutes, or until the jasmine flavor is strong but not bitter. Strain the liquid through a fine mesh sieve.

Add the lettuce, carrots, and peas to the pot with the onions, along with the jasmine infusion and a little salt. Bring to a boil and cook for 2 minutes, or until the lettuce is cooked but still has texture and the peas are done.

TO SERVE: Ladle the broth and vegetables into warm bowls and top with the chicken, either whole or sliced. Serve immediately.

Plum-Jasmine Jam

MAKES 3 TO 4 CUPS

In this dish, plums are simmered with vanilla for a deep sweetness and finished with a jasmine infusion. The resulting jam is sweet and tart, with a fresh summery flavor. It will keep for several weeks in the refrigerator.

3 pounds ripe plums, preferably Santa Rosa or Mariposa (about 13 to 15)

1/2 vanilla bean

3 tablespoons apple pectin

1/4 cup sugar

2 teaspoons jasmine pearls

1/2 cup very hot water

Salt

Score the plums on the bottom with a small "x." Bring a pot of water to a boil and blanch the plums for 10 seconds. Remove to a plate to cool. Peel the plums and cut the flesh away from the pits. Dice the plums into 1/2 -inch pieces and place in a nonreactive pot. Split the vanilla bean lengthwise and scrape the seeds into the pot, then add the pod as well. Add the pectin and sugar. Cook the plums over medium heat for 20 to 25 minutes, until they are very tender. Don't overcook or the fruit will lose its freshness.

While the plums are cooking, combine the jasmine pearls and hot water in a cup and let steep for 8 to 10 minutes, until the flavor and aroma is very strong. Strain through a fine mesh sieve.

Add the jasmine infusion to the cooked plums and cook for 2 minutes more to let the flavors meld. Add a pinch of salt, discard the vanilla pod, cool, and refrigerate.

ROSE ~

Rose *absolute,* like jasmine, is a *middle note* that forgives all indiscretions and brings out the best in the other notes with its full-bodied, unthreatening beauty. Just as there are avid gardeners who can distinguish among the many varieties of rose just by smelling them, an experienced perfumer can differentiate among rose absolutes from India, Egypt, Morocco, France, Bulgaria, and Russia. It has even been noted that the roses on a given bush smell different at different times of day, and the intensity of the scent increases before a storm. Rose, considered an aphrodisiac, is thought to drive away melancholy and lift the heart.

In the kitchen, rose integrates perfectly into a wide range of dishes. Although rose marries more naturally with desserts, the aroma and flavor of rose added to a traditional savory butter sauce is memorable. The recipes here use rosewater, a *hydrosol* that can be found in many Middle Eastern markets, and Moroccan rose absolute, the most beautiful of all of the rose essences.

IN THE EVERYDAY KITCHEN: Add a few drops of rose absolute to cake batter to make a wonderfully frangrant cake, or use it to flavor pastry or buttercream.

ROSE, NEROLI, AND FRANKINCENSE FACE ELIXIR

This restorative elixir is intended for dry or aging skin. Rose absolute soothes and moisturizes, frankincense smooths wrinkles and gives lift to the skin, and neroli helps to regenerate cells. The apricot kernel oil, squalene, and rose hip seed oil are easily absorbed into the skin, and each has emollient and rejuvenating qualities. Apply before going to bed.

10 milliliters apricot kernel oil

2¹/₂ milliliters squalene

2¹/₂ milliliters rose hip seed oil

8 drops frankincense essential oil

8 drops rose absolute

4 drops neroli essential oil

Combine the apricot kernel oil with the squalene and rose hip seed oil. Stir with a stirring stick. Add the remaining essences. Store in an attractive small bottle and use within 3 months. Shake before using.

Strawberries Marinated in Rosewater

SERVES 8

This is probably the easiest recipe in the book, yet it is one of the most satisfying. Serve the strawberries by themselves with some of the juices ladled over them, or with sweetened yogurt or fromage blanc.

10 cups washed and quartered strawberries (about 5 pints)

2 tablespoons rosewater

Sugar

Toss the strawberries with the rosewater and sugar to taste. Hold in a covered container in the refrigerator for at least 3 hours, but preferably not more than 6. Gently stir from time to time. Bring to room temperature before serving.

Sea Bass with
Rosewater Beurre Blanc and Porcini

SERVES 8

The combination of a mild, white-fleshed fish with mushrooms and butter sauce is tried and true, but the addition of earthy porcini and delicate rosewater creates a new and compelling interplay of flavors and aromas. The recipe uses what seems to be a shocking amount of rosewater, but since the rosewater is very fat soluble, it takes quite a bit to get to the point that its flavor and aroma start to become evident. It is best to add the rosewater in increments, because it varies in strength from brand to brand.

The sauce is basically a classic beurre blanc, or "white butter" sauce, to which rosewater is added at the end. A beurre blanc is a bit of a trick sauce, an emulsion of butter and little else, with nothing to bind or stabilize it. Use a pot that is not very wide and do the reduction at a moderate heat. When it is ready, cool the reduction down for a moment until very warm but not hot.

Start the emulsion off the heat with several pieces of butter and return the pan to low heat. Add more butter while there are still several pieces of half-melted butter in the pot, because the critical mass of the butter will help the stability of the sauce in the beginning stages of the emulsion, when the sauce is weakest. If the sauce breaks, add a tablespoon of rosewater to a clean pan, heat it, whisk in enough cold butter to make a firm emulsion, and then slowly whisk back in the broken sauce, which will bind with the good emulsion. Flavoring such as rosewater should be added to the finished sauce. Beurre blancs can also be flavored with thyme, chopped capers and lemon, or parsley.

4 tablespoons unsalted butter	1 medium yellow onion, thinly sliced (about 7 ounces unpeeled)
12 ounces fresh porcini, cleaned and sliced (see Note, page 130)	Eight 5-ounce sea bass fillets
Salt and freshly ground black pepper	Rosewater Beurre Blanc (recipe follows)

Melt 3 tablespoons of the butter over medium heat and add the porcini. Cook, covered, for 2 minutes, stirring occasionally. Season with salt. Continue to cook, stirring occasionally, until the porcini are tender and fragrant. Hold warm.

While the porcini are cooking, cook the onion in the remaining tablespoon of butter, covered, with salt over a gentle heat, stirring occasionally, until tender. Add it to the pot with the porcini and stir to combine. If you are making the porcini and onion ahead of time, you can cool them by spreading them out on a plate and refrigerating them.

Season the bass with salt on both sides and black pepper only on the non-presentation side. Cook the fish in a steamer set over lightly simmering water until just cooked, white on the outside and translucent in the center. The cooking time will depend on the thickness of the fish; generally it takes 5 to 10 minutes.

TO SERVE: While the fish is cooking, heat the porcini and onions, season them with freshly ground black pepper, and mound them in the center of eight warm plates. When the fish is cooked, set a fillet on each pile of porcini, and ladle over 2 tablespoons of rosewater beurre blanc. Serve immediately.

ROSEWATER BEURRE BLANC
1/3 cup dry white wine
1 medium shallot, peeled and sliced
10 peppercorns

9 ounces cold unsalted butter, cut into 1/2-ounce cubes
1/2 cup rosewater
Salt

In a nonreactive pot, reduce the white wine, shallot, and peppercorns over low-medium heat until only 1 tablespoon of liquid remains. Remove from the heat, cool slightly until it is warm but not hot, add 7 cubes of the cold butter into the pot and begin whisking. Return to low heat, and when the butter is partially melted, add 2 more pieces. Repeat this process until all of the butter is incorporated. Strain through a basket strainer into a small pot and add the rosewater a little at a time, tasting after each addition. The rose flavor should be clear, but not so strong as to be soapy or unpleasant. Season with salt and hold warm by placing the pot into a larger pot half filled with warm—but not hot—water. The sauce can be held warm for an hour or so, but it is best to use it as soon as possible.

Rose and Ginger Soufflé

SERVES 8

This soufflé is based on yogurt instead of the traditional pastry cream, which gives the soufflé incredible lightness and a subtle tanginess. It is easy to make, and the aroma of the rose intermingled with the ginger is unforgettable.

The idea that soufflés need to be baked at a high temperature in order to achieve height is incorrect. Soufflés are best baked at a lower temperature because, like any protein, slower cooking allows the eggs to set more softly, creating a more delicate texture. The lightness of this soufflé makes it seem as if you are eating nothing but the pure aroma.

Unsalted butter, for buttering baking dishes

Sugar, for dusting baking dishes

1 cup plain whole-milk yogurt

2 large egg yolks

1 tablespoon fresh blood orange juice (you can substitute regular fresh orange juice)

10 drops Moroccan rose absolute

13 drops ginger essential oil

1 cup large egg whites

¾ cup confectioners' sugar

Salt

Butter and sugar eight 4-ounce soufflé molds or ovenproof ceramic cups. In a mixing bowl, combine the yogurt, egg yolks, blood orange juice, and essences.

Preheat the oven to 325°F. In a mixer fitted with the whisk attachment, beat the whites on low speed with half of the sugar and a pinch of salt until they form soft peaks. Add the rest of the sugar and continue beating until the whites form stiff peaks.

Carefully fold ⅓ of the whites into the yogurt base. Do not overmix. Fold in the rest of the whites until just combined and ladle into the soufflé molds. Fill the molds completely and then run your thumb around the top edge of the rim to create a slight indentation in the soufflé mixture. Bake until set but still moist inside, about 10 minutes. Serve hot in the soufflé molds.

Earthy

Coffee
Cèpe
Truffle
Green Tea

Yellow Corn Pudding Glazed with White Truffle Butter (page 138).
OPPOSITE: Porcini Tart with Walnuts and Wild Arugula (page 132).

OPPOSITE, FROM LEFT: cocoa powder, coffee beans, cognac, black truffle, chocolate block.
ABOVE: Green Tea Panna Cotta (page 144).

COFFEE ~

Everyone knows the smell of a freshly brewed cup of coffee—rich, familiar, and evocative. Coffee *absolute* is an earthy, dark *middle note* of high odor intensity that is used in minute amounts to balance out blends that are cloying and without depth. It marries well with ylang-ylang and fir absolute.

Coffee as a flavor makes a wonderful partner in a dish, imparting a mysterious, haunting quality and blending so well with everything around it that it becomes transformed itself. Because of its bitter, astringent nature it needs sugar to round out the flavors.

IN THE EVERYDAY KITCHEN: Add an ounce or two of brewed coffee to braised chicken or game birds as they cook. The coffee will create a subtle background note of earthy bitterness, which is especially welcome with sweet accompaniments, such as sweet potatoes or parsnips. You can also try flavoring crème brulée with coffee absolute, or add a few drops to the Chocolate-Cinnamon Caramels (page 152) in place of the cinnamon essential oil.

COFFEE COLOGNE SPRAY

This cologne smells especially delicious on a man. The scent of coffee creates a rich foundation with the sweet heaviness of patchouli and the caramel scent of Peru balsam. Only a small amount of coffee is used so as to not overwhelm the floral heart of neroli and rose. Extending the sweetness are the grand fir and pink grapefruit top notes.

30 milliliters grape alcohol

8 drops vanilla absolute

8 drops blond tobacco absolute

6 drops patchouli essential oil

8 drops Peru balsam essential oil

7 drops coffee absolute

8 drops neroli essential oil

10 drops rose absolute

8 drops grand fir essential oil

8 drops pink grapefruit essential oil

8 drops bitter orange essential oil

Pour the grape alcohol into a beaker, measuring cup, or small glass. Drop in the essences, beginning with the vanilla, and stir with a stirring stick. Stir to mix completely. Pour into a bottle with a secure lid and let marry for a week or more. Before using, strain the mixture through a plastic coffee filter fitted with unbleached paper. After filtration, this cologne will be golden brown and bright like a topaz. Decant into a spray bottle.

Bittersweet Chocolate–Coffee Sauce

MAKES ABOUT 3 CUPS

This simple recipe combines two classic flavors—coffee and bittersweet chocolate. It takes only about 10 minutes to make and can be kept refrigerated for a month or more. Drizzle the warmed sauce on vanilla or chocolate ice cream, use it as a sauce for chocolate cake, or as a dip for cookies.

2 cups freshly brewed coffee

10 ounces chopped bittersweet chocolate, preferably Valrhona Extra Bitter (see Sources, page 201)

3 tablespoons unsalted butter

3 tablespoons sugar

Salt

In a nonreactive pot, bring the coffee to a boil over medium-high heat. Off the heat, add the chocolate, whisk until the chocolate is melted, and return to the heat for about 20 seconds, whisking constantly, until the sauce boils. Remove from the heat and whisk in the butter, sugar, and 2 pinches of salt. Cool and refrigerate if not needed immediately.

Pork Chop with Coffee-Fig Sauce

SERVES 8

This unusual combination of sweet, sour, and bitter flavors was inspired by the classic diner dish of redeye gravy, in which a quick pan sauce flavored with coffee is served with sautéed ham. Here fresh figs give the sauce sweetness and body to balance the bitterness of the coffee; both in turn are cut with balsamic vinegar and lime, and rounded out with a sweet-savory puree of parsnips and potatoes. The aroma of the coffee integrates so well with the figs and pork that it creates an elusive scent, familiar yet mysterious.

6 large or 8 small fresh figs	Good-quality instant espresso
1 to 2 tablespoons sugar	3 tablespoons unsalted butter
Salt and freshly ground black pepper	Parsnip-Potato Puree (recipe follows)
8 pork chops	Coffee-Fig Sauce (recipe follows)

Trim the stems off of the figs and cut them in half. Lay the figs cut side up on a sheet pan and sprinkle them evenly with sugar, and about one-quarter as much salt as sugar.

Bake the figs at 300°F until they swell, leak just a drop or two of their juices, and are tender but not falling apart, about 15 minutes. Cool, dice into ⅓-inch pieces, and reserve.

Season the pork chops with salt and pepper, and sprinkle them on both sides with a generous amount of instant espresso. Melt the butter in one or two pans over moderate heat until bubbling. Cook the pork chops in the butter, allowing the butter to brown but not burn, basting the meat occasionally with the butter. When done, remove the chops to a plate to rest for a few minutes.

TO SERVE: While the pork is cooking, heat the Parsnip-Potato Puree, and in a separate pot, heat the Coffee-Fig Sauce and the roasted figs together. Spoon a pile of the puree onto each plate, lean a pork chop against it, and then spoon some of the sauce next to the pork chop. Sprinkle the whole plate with a little instant espresso and serve immediately.

PARSNIP-POTATO PUREE

2 cups peeled and sliced parsnips
(3 to 6 parsnips, 1 pound)

2 cups peeled and sliced russet potatoes
(1 to 3 potatoes, 1½ pounds)

¾ cup whole milk

3 tablespoons unsalted butter

Salt

Simmer the parsnips and potatoes in separate pots of salted water until both are very tender. Drain them well, combine, and pass them through a food mill. Return the mixture to the cooking pot.

Heat the milk and butter together and pour slowly into the parsnip-potato mixture, stirring constantly. When they are well combined, season with salt and set aside, covered, for up to 30 minutes. You can also puree the vegetables an hour or two before and hold in a covered pot, then add the milk and butter just before serving.

COFFEE-FIG SAUCE

Scant ⅓ cup sugar

3 ounces balsamic vinegar

2 pounds fresh figs

1½ cups freshly brewed coffee

1 teaspoon fresh lime juice

Salt

While the parsnips and potatoes are cooking, caramelize the sugar in a heavy-bottomed saucepan over medium-high heat until deep brown in color. Carefully add the balsamic vinegar (it will splatter), then the figs and coffee, and simmer until the figs are very tender.

Puree the figs and liquid in a blender and pass through a fine mesh sieve. Add the lime juice and season with salt and more sugar as necessary. The flavor should be balanced: sweet, sour, and bitter, with the salt sharpening the flavors. If the sauce seems too sweet, add a bit of salt first. If there is then enough salt but the sauce is still too sweet, add a splash more balsamic vinegar and/or lime. Hold warm.

Coffee-Date Ice Cream with Candied Orange

SERVES 8

Coffee and date make a compelling union of bitter and sweet, and it is hard in the end to know where one leaves off and the other begins. The pectin in the dates acts as a binder for the ice cream, so despite the lack of eggs in the recipe, the ice cream turns out incredibly creamy. The ice cream is a bit sweet, and it needs a surprising amount of salt to balance and sharpen the flavors. You can make the ice cream a day in advance; if it sets too much, leave it in the refrigerator for ten to fifteen minutes before serving to soften it. The candied orange peels can be made days in advance and will keep for at least a month in the refrigerator.

COFFEE-DATE ICE CREAM

2 cups freshly brewed coffee

12 ounces pitted dried dates

1/2 cup sugar

1 1/2 teaspoons minced fresh ginger

2 cups heavy cream

Salt

CANDIED ORANGE PEELS

4 oranges

4 cups water

1 cup sugar

FOR THE ICE CREAM: Simmer the coffee and dates together with the sugar and the ginger, covered, until the dates are softened, about 15 minutes. Cool and puree in a blender with the cream until smooth. Strain through a fine mesh sieve and season to taste with salt. Freeze in an ice cream machine according to the manufacturer's directions.

FOR THE CANDIED ORANGE PEELS: Cut the peel away from the orange in segments, cutting from top to bottom, and keeping the peel as thick as possible. You should see the exposed orange flesh when you are done. Cut the orange peel lengthwise into strips about 1/4 inch thick, and boil in 3 cups of water for 1 hour to 1 hour and 15 minutes, adding water as needed, until the white pith has turned translucent and the peel has lost most of its bitterness. Drain the peels and put them back in the pot with the remaining 1 cup water and the sugar. Simmer for 15 minutes or until sweet. Cool and refrigerate.

TO SERVE: Put some of the candied orange peels in a chilled bowl and top with a scoop of the ice cream. Serve immediately.

CÈPE ~

Cèpe *absolute* is the essence of wild mushrooms—intense, sexy, and earthy. Used in very small amounts, this earthy aroma grounds any blend that's too ethereal or lacks depth. Cèpe absolute blends well with strong florals like tuberose, orange flower, and jasmine.

Cèpes, more commonly known as porcini, grow wild in the spring and fall. They range from thumb to fist size, with large white stems and smaller brown caps. They are, along with morels, the most iconic and revered of all mushrooms, with their indescribably sweet, deep aroma and flavor of earth and forest. When buying porcini, avoid any with small holes in the stems, an indication of worms, which are harmless but mean the mushrooms are less than fresh. They should be firm to the touch, and the cap should show no sign of decay. Cèpes work best in simple settings where their special flavor can shine; like all mushrooms, they have a strong affinity for eggs.

IN THE EVERYDAY KITCHEN: Make a meat loaf with veal instead of beef and season it with cèpe, add some cèpe absolute to mashed potatoes, or use it to enhance the flavor of a mushroom soup.

The heaviness of the cèpe absolute is balanced by the light but sweet *base notes* of sandalwood and benzoin. The intensity of the tuberose has some of the fungal quality of the cèpes and adds a voluptuous, floral quality.

15 milliliters ethyl alcohol

4 drops cèpe absolute

12 drops sandalwood essential oil

15 drops benzoin resin

12 drops tuberose absolute

8 drops rose absolute

15 drops bergamot essential oil

9 drops bois de rose essential oil

7 drops pink grapefruit essential oil

Put the ethyl alcohol in a beaker, drop in the essences, and stir with a stirring stick. Pour into a bottle and let marry for a week or more. Decant into a small bottle, preferably one with a ground glass stopper. Over time, the cèpe and tuberose meld into a voluptuous scent that resembles neither.

Glazed Porcini

SERVES 8

With their focused intensity of flavor and aroma, glazed porcini can be served on their own as part of a multicourse meal. They also work well as a side dish with roast chicken, steak, veal, or a strongly flavored white fish such as monkfish.

1 stick (4 ounces) unsalted butter

1½ pounds fresh porcini, cleaned and cut into large pieces (see Note)

Salt and freshly ground black pepper

1 cup Mushroom Stock (page 198)

10 drops cèpe absolute

In a wide sauté pan, melt the butter over medium heat and add the porcini. Season with salt after they are completely covered in the butter (otherwise the salt will bounce off of the dry mushrooms). Cook the porcini, stirring frequently, until they are nicely browned and tender, about 10 minutes. Add the mushroom stock and reduce, stirring frequently, until the mushrooms are glazed. Add the cèpe absolute and correct the seasoning with salt and black pepper. Divide among warm bowls and serve immediately.

NOTE: To clean the porcini, scrape the dirt off with a paring knife, then wipe with a damp towel and dry on a clean towel. Remove the large green gills on the underside of the cap.

Porcini-Lemongrass Consommé

SERVES 8

The brightness of the lemongrass and the brooding depth of porcini make for a light yet richly flavored consommé. This is wonderful sipped out of cups, or as a broth for chicken or fish, perhaps accompanied by sautéed porcini. Don't cook the lemongrass too long or it will lose its freshness of flavor.

1 stalk lemongrass, sliced

1 quart Mushroom Stock (page 198)

1 quart Vegetable Stock (page 197)

1 ounce dried (1 cup plus 1 tablespoon), porcini, wiped clean

Salt

Bring all of the ingredients to a boil. Lower the heat to a bare simmer and continue cooking for 10 minutes. Remove from the heat and let it stand infusing, warm, for an additional 20 minutes, or until the flavors of the porcini and lemongrass are clear and direct. Strain through a fine mesh sieve and correct seasoning. Either serve immediately or cool and reheat later, but the aromas and flavors will start to fade after the day it is made.

Porcini Tart with Walnuts and Wild Arugula

SERVES 8, pictured on page 121

The tart is easy to make and fun to eat, with its play of different textures and flavors. A prebaked pastry shell is spread with mushroom puree, topped with sautéed mushrooms and walnuts, and heated briefly in the oven; finally, wild arugula is scattered over the top. The aroma of porcini that is released when the tarts are brought to the table is wonderful. All of the different components can be made early in the day and then assembled just before serving.

Making puff pastry at home is a challenging endeavor. It is easier to buy it from a local bakery, specialty store, or supermarket in frozen sheets. Wild arugula, which is in season at the same times as fresh porcini, can be found at farmers' markets, specialty stores, or by mail order (see Sources, page 201). It has a more peppery, intense flavor than common arugula. You can substitute baby arugula, or mature arugula cut into strips.

8 puff pastry pieces, cut in 4-by-3-inch rectangles	4 tablespoons unsalted butter
¼ cup walnuts	Salt and freshly ground black pepper
1¼ pounds (18 ounces) cleaned fresh porcini	10 drops cèpe absolute
	1 cup wild arugula leaves

FOR THE PUFF PASTRY: Set the puff pastry rectangles on parchment paper on a sheet tray. Refrigerate for 30 minutes.

Meanwhile, toast the walnuts. Preheat the oven to 325°F. Spread the walnuts on a sheet pan and toast, stirring often, until golden brown and fragrant, about 15 minutes. Cool and cut into ¼-inch pieces. Reserve.

Remove the pastry from the refrigerator. Put something heat resistant about ½ inch high along all four sides of the sheet tray, about 1 inch in from the edge. Dinner knives work well. Put a piece of parchment paper over the dough and the knives, and then another sheet tray of the same size on top of the first. It will rest on top of the dinner knives and provide a barrier so that the puff pastry shells will all rise to an even ½ inch.

Bake for 25 minutes and then remove the top sheet pan. Continue to bake for another 20 minutes or so, until the pastry is a deep golden brown. Remove the sheet pan, let the pastry cool, then wrap it tightly in plastic wrap. This can be done at any point earlier in the day.

Slice 8 ounces of the porcini and cook them in 2 tablespoons of butter with salt, in a covered saucepan, until very tender, about 25 minutes. Process the mushrooms in a food processor with the cèpe absolute. It should become mostly smooth, but still retain some texture. Adjust seasoning and reserve.

Preheat the oven to 325°F. Dice the remaining porcini into ½-inch cubes. Melt the remaining 2 tablespoons butter in a large sauté pan, and when the butter starts to bubble, add the mushrooms and cook over medium-high heat, stirring often, until they are browned and tender, seasoning with salt as they cook. Cool on a plate and reserve.

TO SERVE: Spread an even layer of the mushroom puree on each tart shell. Sprinkle the sautéed porcini over each tart, then the toasted walnuts. Bake for 4 to 5 minutes, until hot.

Grind black pepper over each tart and sprinkle with a generous amount of wild arugula. Serve immediately.

TRUFFLE ~

There is no truffle essential oil or *absolute,* so the best way to access the flavor and aroma of truffles is with truffle oil, which is widely available in both white and black varieties (see Sources, page 201). Be careful when purchasing the oils because the quality varies wildly, and some can have an unpleasant petrol or chemical odor. White truffle oil makes a beautiful base for solid perfume. You can temper its gamy quality by combining it with citrus essential oils.

When you cook with truffle oils, the aroma and flavor dissipate during prolonged cooking, so use them in a vinaigrette, or drizzle them over foods to finish the dish. Fresh truffles, both white and black, should be clean (otherwise you are paying for very expensive dirt), firm, and so aromatic that they fill a room. Rub them lightly with a brush to clean them, and then rub them with a damp cloth to remove any trace of grit. Store them wrapped in a paper towel in a closed container in the refrigerator until you need them, but use them as soon as possible as they are quite perishable.

> **IN THE EVERYDAY KITCHEN:** Truffles have a strong affinity for potatoes, so try adding either black or white truffle oil to a new-potato salad or a potato-leek soup. Try drizzling white truffle oil over scrambled eggs with Parmesan, or use black truffle oil to scent a sauté of wild mushrooms. The Balsamic–Black Truffle Vinaigrette (page 136) makes a nice complement to grilled meats.

WHITE TRUFFLE AND BLOOD ORANGE
SOLID PERFUME

Most specialty grocery stores carry white truffle oil. The fruitiness of the olive oil tempers the earthy and penetrating aroma of the truffle. (Buy only the smallest bottle, as you'll need very little.) The coffee bolsters and gives body to the earthiness of the truffle, and blood orange contributes a radiance that modulates the heaviness of the blend.

5 milliliters white truffle oil

6 drops coffee absolute

33 drops blood orange essential oil

1/2 heaping teaspoon grated beeswax

Mix the white truffle, coffee, and blood orange oils together in a small beaker. Heat the beeswax in a small pan or dish over low heat on the stove or on a laboratory hot plate. When the beeswax has melted, add the oils and heat, stirring with a stirring stick, for just a few seconds. Pour the mixture into a jar or compact, cover immediately, and let it set undisturbed for 15 minutes.

Mixed Chicory Salad with Balsamic–Black Truffle Vinaigrette

SERVES 8

Chicories are a family of bitter lettuces, which include endive, frisée, escarole, and dandelion greens, as well as some unusual varieties of radicchio that are starting to show up, such as *pan di zucchero* and *radicchio di Treviso*. Buy whatever looks best at the market (farmers' or otherwise), but try to get as much variety as possible. If you want to make this with fresh black truffles, substitute a golden-green olive oil (Ligurian olive oils are best) for the truffle oil, and shave the truffles into the salad just before tossing. Use at least one ounce of truffle to get the full effect.

BALSAMIC–BLACK TRUFFLE VINAIGRETTE

Salt

⅓ cup good-quality balsamic vinegar

2 teaspoons fresh lemon juice

⅓ cup black truffle oil

White pepper

4 quarts mixed chicories, cleaned and trimmed (see Note)

Salt and freshly ground black pepper

FOR THE VINAIGRETTE: In a small mixing bowl, dissolve some salt in the balsamic vinegar and lemon juice. Whisk in the truffle oil and adjust the seasoning with salt and white pepper.

TO SERVE: In a large salad mixing bowl, toss the chicories with some of the vinaigrette (you may not need all of it), and the salt and black pepper. Divide among eight plates or bowls.

NOTE: When trimming chicories, the most important goals are to remove any tough pieces, such as ribs and stems, and to cut the lettuce into bite-size pieces. For endive, you might want to simply slice the leaves crosswise; for frisée, you can cut off the green tops (they tend to be tough), remove the core, and then pull apart the remaining leaves; for escarole, remove the tough outer leaves and core and cut the leaves the lettuce into wide strips; for radicchio, remove the core, cut the leaves into eighths, then separate the leaves; for dandelion greens, separate each leaf and, using a sharp knife, cut along either side of the rib, which will create many small, tender pieces. (Use your best judgment and sample the pieces as you go along. If they taste good, use them; if they don't taste good, discard them.)

Morels and Spring Vegetables
with Black Truffle Oil

SERVES 8

Mid to late spring, when the morels are in season, is also when you can find spring onions and green garlic. Spring onions and green garlic are vegetables in their youth, before they grow a papery skin and are harvested for storage. They usually still have green tops attached, and their flavor is sweet and mild. Here they add depth and body to a stew of morels that is finished with butter and black truffle oil.

2 cups sliced spring onions
(4 to 8 onions) (or 2 medium
yellow onions, peeled and sliced)

2 tablespoons minced green garlic
(or 2 teaspoons regular garlic)

6 tablespoons unsalted butter

Salt and freshly ground black pepper

1 cup Champagne

5 cups fresh morels

1 cup Mushroom Stock (page 198)

3½ cups fresh peas (about 3 pounds in the pod)

½ cup black truffle oil
(or ½ cups chopped black truffle)

In a nonreactive pot, cook the onions and garlic in 2 tablespoons of the butter with salt, covered, until tender.

Add the Champagne and reduce by a third, then add the morels, mushroom stock, and more salt, if necessary. Cook at a slow simmer, covered, until the morels are tender, about 10 minutes.

Add the peas and cook for 2 minutes more, until the peas are just tender.

Stir in the remaining 4 tablespoons butter to create a smooth sauce. Adjust the seasoning with salt and black pepper. If you are using chopped truffles instead of the truffle oil, stir them in at this point and let them sit for a minute, covered. The warmth of the broth will release their flavor and aroma.

TO SERVE: Ladle the stew into warm bowls. Drizzle 1 tablespoon of black truffle oil, if using, over each bowl and serve immediately.

Yellow Corn Pudding Glazed with White Truffle Butter

SERVES 8, pictured on page 120

This is a glorious expression of midsummer, when corn is intensely sweet and flavorful. Here bread pudding is reworked into an elegant, sensually textured combination of corn custard and brioche, which is baked in the oven until set and glazed with a sauce made from corn juice and butter scented with white truffle oil. Make the corn stock first, as you will need it to prepare the corn custard. You will need eight 4-ounce ovenproof molds or ramekins.

CUSTARD BASE AND PUDDING

2 cups Corn Stock (recipe follows)

3 ounces leeks, white and light green parts only, cut in ¼-inch squares

1 tablespoon unsalted butter, plus more for buttering ramekins

Salt

10¾ ounces corn kernels, all silk removed

½ teaspoon chopped fresh thyme

½ to 1 cup heavy cream

2 large eggs

3 large egg yolks

White pepper

1 cup brioche cut in ¼-inch cubes

White Truffle Butter (recipe follows)

Prepare the corn stock.

Cook the leeks in 1½ teaspoons of the butter with salt, covered, until tender. Spread out on a plate to cool. Cook 5 ounces of the corn in the remaining 1½ teaspoons of butter with salt, covered, until tender. Spread the corn on top of the leeks to cool. Sprinkle the chopped thyme over the corn and leeks.

Simmer the corn stock and the remaining 5¾ ounces of corn with salt, covered, for about 45 minutes, until the corn is tender. Puree the corn and corn stock together and pass the liquid through a fine mesh sieve. Measure the liquid and add enough cream to the puree to bring to 2 cups.

In a mixing bowl, whisk the whole eggs and yolks to combine. Whisk in the corn puree, adjust the seasoning with salt and white pepper, and pass the mixture through a fine mesh sieve.

Mix the cooled leeks, corn, and thyme together, adjusting the seasoning with salt as necessary. Stir them into the custard base.

Preheat the oven to 300°F. Butter the ramekins. Combine the custard base and the brioche, fill the prepared molds with the mixture, and place in a deep roasting pan. Put the roasting pan in the oven and fill the pan with hot water halfway up the sides of the molds. Cover with aluminum foil and bake until they feel set and the tops swell just a touch, 45 to 50 minutes. The puddings will keep at room temperature for up to 2 hours.

TO SERVE: If necessary, rewarm the puddings by placing them in a hot water bath in a 300°F oven. (You can check if the insides are hot by inserting a metal skewer or knife into the center of a pudding and feeling it.) Run a paring knife around the inside of the ramekins to loosen the puddings, and unmold them onto warm plates. Glaze with enough of the white truffle butter to coat the puddings and pool on the bottom of the plate a bit, and serve immediately. If using fresh white truffles, omit the truffle oil from the sauce, and shave the fresh truffles generously over the puddings after saucing.

CORN STOCK

6 ears of corn, shucked

5 cups water

Cut the kernels off of 4 ears and reserve them for the corn custard base and the corn juice. Cut the corn cobs and remaining 2 ears of corn in half, place them in a pot, cover them with the water, and simmer until the liquid is reduced by half and tastes intensely of corn, about 2 hours. Make sure you have at least 2 cups. This can be done the day before. Store the stock in the refrigerator.

WHITE TRUFFLE BUTTER

1 cup corn juice (see Note)

6 tablespoons unsalted butter, cut into small pieces

2 tablespoons plus 2 teaspoons white truffle oil

Salt

White pepper

In a nonreactive pot, gently heat the corn juice, stirring constantly, until the natural starches in the corn cause it to thicken. If it seems too thick, add a little corn stock to thin it out. Whisk in the butter a few pieces at a time until the sauce is smooth and well emulsified. Add the white truffle oil and season to taste with salt and white pepper. If you need to hold this warm, use a warm (not hot) water bath.

NOTE: For the corn juice, cut away the kernels from the cob and juice them with a vegetable juicer according to the manufacturer's instructions. For 1 cup of juice, you will need about 2 cups of kernels, or 1 to 2 ears. You can also puree the corn with a few tablespoons of corn stock in a food processor and pass the mixture through a fine mesh sieve. You will need a little extra corn for this method, as it is not as efficient as a vegetable juicer.

GREEN TEA~

Rich, delicate, dry, but slightly sweet, green tea *absolute* evokes the emotions surrounding the ritual of steeping a cup of tea. This cool and soft *base note* complements less assertive *top* and *middle notes* of any blend and marries well with orange, light floral, and green notes.

Green tea is used in the food recipes in two forms, as a traditional tea and in a powdered form called *macha* in Japanese. Most high-quality tea purveyors carry powdered green tea, but you can also order it by mail (see Sources, page 201). The slight bitterness of green tea pairs well with sweet flavors, especially honey, and it adds a haunting, nutty flavor when infused into savory soups and broths.

> **IN THE EVERYDAY KITCHEN:** Steep green tea and orange zest in warm milk, strain, then use the milk to make a dessert sauce such as crème anglaise. Add a little brewed green tea to a meat or poultry sauce to add an earthy, nutty flavor.

This solid perfume is a perfect marriage. The comforting scent of green tea, complicated and slightly astringent, is balanced and sweetened by the addition of citrus scents, rose, and coriander. This scent can be worn by itself or layered over other perfumes.

1/8 teaspoon green tea absolute

5 milliliters jojoba essential oil

5 drops neroli essential oil

2 drops rose absolute

2 drops coriander essential oil

5 drops bitter orange essential oil

3 drops sweet orange essential oil

Heaping 1/2 teaspoon grated beeswax

Combine the green tea absolute with the jojoba using a stirring stick. The green tea will not mix thoroughly with the jojoba oil, but later, as the mixture is heated, it will disperse more evenly. Add the drops of neroli, rose, coriander, and bitter and sweet orange essential oils to the jojoba–green tea mixture. Put this aside. Heat the beeswax in a nonmetal pan on a hot plate. When the beeswax has melted, add the oils and heat, stirring with a skewer or chopstick, for just a few seconds. Some sediment is inevitable from the green tea. Pour the mixture into a compact, cover immediately, and let it set undisturbed for 15 minutes.

Green Tea–Pistachio Crusted Cod

SERVES 8

Here green tea powder and pistachios are blended to form a mixture that tops baked cod. Sweet and sour turnips, cooked with honey and lemon juice until tender, balance the earthiness and astringency of the crust; the slow baking keeps the fish moist. You can substitute other white-fleshed fish for the cod, such as halibut or bass.

continued

HONEY-LEMON GLAZED TURNIPS

2 pounds turnips

2 tablespoons unsalted butter

2 medium yellow onions, peeled, quartered, and thinly sliced

1/2 cup water

5 tablespoons honey

1/2 cup plus 1 tablespoon fresh lemon juice

Salt

GREEN TEA–PISTACHIO CRUST

3/4 cup raw pistachios

1 tablespoon powdered green tea

1 tablespoon water

1 teaspoon sugar

Zest of 1 lemon, finely chopped

3 tablespoons melted unsalted butter

1/4 cup dried bread crumbs

Salt and freshly ground black pepper

Eight 5-ounce pieces cod fillet

Unsalted butter, for baking pan

Salt and freshly ground black pepper

FOR THE TURNIPS: Peel, quarter, and slice the turnips into 1/4-inch-thick pieces. Melt 1 tablespoon of the butter over medium-low heat in a heavy-bottomed nonreactive saucepan and add the onions. Cook, covered, until tender. Add the turnips, water, honey, and lemon juice. Season with the salt and cook, covered, stirring occasionally, until the turnips are just tender. Remove the lid, add the remaining tablespoon of butter, and reduce the liquid over medium heat until the turnips are glazed. Remove from heat.

FOR THE CRUST: While the turnips are cooking, puree the pistachios, green tea, water, and sugar in a food processor until the pistachios are in small pieces, about 15 seconds. Add the lemon zest, melted butter, bread crumbs, salt, and pepper, and puree 10 seconds more. Adjust seasoning as needed with salt and pepper.

Preheat the oven to 325°F. Season the cod lightly with salt and pepper on both sides. Pat a thin layer of crust over the top of the fish. Place the cod on a buttered piece of parchment set on a sheet pan, and bake until the fish is firm but not hard to the touch and translucent inside, 5 to 10 minutes depending on the thickness of the fillet.

TO SERVE: While the fish is cooking, divide the turnips among eight plates. Place the fish on top of the turnips and serve immediately.

Green Tea–Scented Chicken Soup

SERVES 8

This is another classic dish with a twist: the homey comfort of chicken soup infused with the aroma and flavor of green tea. The key here is a high-quality homemade chicken stock, because it is the soul of the dish. I recommend making the stock the day before so that the fat will harden and rise to the surface and can be easily removed. Served over rice, this makes a satisfying main dish.

6 boneless skinless chicken breasts, diced into ¹/₂-inch pieces

Salt and freshly ground black pepper

9 cups Chicken Stock (page 199)

3 carrots, peeled and sliced

1 fennel bulb, cored, quartered, and sliced into ¹/₂-inch pieces

3 leeks, white and light green parts only, split lengthwise and cut into ¹/₂-inch pieces

¹/₄ cup green tea leaves

1 tablespoon fresh lemon juice

Season the chicken with salt and a little black pepper and let stand, covered, for 20 minutes.

Bring the chicken stock to a light simmer in a large saucepan, and add salt and the vegetables. When the vegetables are tender, add the chicken, cover, and remove from the heat. Let stand for about 5 minutes, until the chicken is barely cooked, then remove the chicken and vegetables to a warm bowl.

Add the green tea to the chicken stock and let steep for about 5 minutes. When the flavor is good, strain through a fine mesh sieve, reheat, and then adjust seasoning with salt and lemon juice.

TO SERVE: Add the vegetables and chicken back to the broth and ladle the soup into bowls.

Green Tea Panna Cotta

SERVES 8, pictured on page 123

Panna cotta is an Italian eggless custard set with gelatin. Here milk and cream are flavored with powdered green tea, whose astringent, nutty flavor is rounded out with honey. Although this can be made the day before, the gelatin will cause the panna cotta to become firmer and less silky. You will need eight individual 4-ounce ramekins. Drizzle the panna cottas with honey before serving if you like.

5¾ sheets gelatin (break off about ¼ of one of the pieces; see Note)

3 cups whole milk

1 cup heavy cream

½ cup honey

2 tablespoons powdered green tea

2 tablespoons sugar

1½ teaspoons fresh lemon juice

Salt

Soften the gelatin in cold water for 5 minutes, and then strain off the water.

Scald the milk and cream together, add the gelatin, stir to dissolve, and cool slightly. Whisk in the honey, powdered green tea, sugar, lemon juice, and salt, and pass through a fine mesh strainer.

Set a mixing bowl over a larger mixing bowl filled with ice water, pour the panna cotta base into the top bowl, and stir gently until it starts to thicken. This will keep the base emulsified and the green tea evenly distributed (this is a good idea any time you are thickening something with gelatin). Divide the mixture into the ramekins and refrigerate until set, 3 hours minimum.

TO SERVE: Unmold the panna cottas: Simply turn the ramekins over onto plates, leave them for 1 minute, then gently lift. If they stick, try gently shaking the molds, and tapping their bottoms, or put the molds in warm water for a few seconds. As a last resort, carefully run a paring knife around the inside of the molds.

NOTE: Sheet gelatin can be bought in most stores that sell baking supplies. It comes in clear sheets that need to be soaked in water for 5 minutes until they are soft, and then drained. The gelatin will then dissolve quickly in warm liquid.

Spicy

Cinnamon
Black Pepper
Ginger
Cumin
Coriander

CLOCKWISE FROM TOP LEFT: Grated beeswax; block of beeswax; cumin essential oil; lavender concrete; Cumin, Lavender, and Oakmoss Solid Perfume (page 165).

OPPOSITE, FROM LEFT: Cumin seeds, coriander seeds, cinnamon sticks and bark, ginger.

CINNAMON ~

The cinnamon tree yields essential oils from its leaves, bark, and root. The most valuable oil comes from the bark. It is a golden color when fresh and becomes red as it ages. Cinnamon possesses a powerful, warm, spicy-sweet character. At first, it smells fresh, fruity, and candylike, but it finishes with a dry, dusty, powdery note. Cinnamon enhances floral blends and enlivens woody notes, but because of its strength, it should be used sparingly.

The recipes use ground cinnamon, which gives a round, measured aroma, and cinnamon bark essential oil, which has driving intensity and complexity, and should be used with great restraint. Though cinnamon is an aroma with warm, comforting associations, such as those of mulled cider or cinnamon rolls, its versatile flavor also works well with exotic spices such as ginger and cardamon.

IN THE EVERYDAY KITCHEN: For heightened cinnamon flavor, use a drop of essential oil instead of ground cinnamon in waffle batter, rice pudding, or French toast (mix it in with the eggs).

This perfume is inspired by the traditional Moroccan spice mixture for cooking, *ras el hanout,* which can contain more than a hundred spices. Just as Moroccan food is a complex layering of savory elements, this balanced blend of spices evokes the multilayered, sensual magic of Moroccan cuisine and culture.

5 drops labdanum absolute	2 drops nutmeg absolute
8 drops myrrh essential oil	2 drops black pepper essential oil
2 drops cardamom absolute	4 drops galangal essential oil
20 drops Bulgarian rose absolute	2 drops saffron essential oil
4 drops cinnamon bark essential oil	4 drops ginger essential oil
2 drops pimento berry essential oil	10 drops bitter orange essential oil
1/8 teaspoon jasmine concrete	15 milliliters ethyl alcohol

Drop the essences into the alcohol and stir with a stirring stick. Pour the mixture into a bottle and let marry for a week or more. Before using, strain the mixture through a plastic coffee filter fitted with unbleached paper. Decant into an attractive bottle, preferably one with a ground glass stopper. Unlike most perfumes, this one mellows with time.

Moroccan Veal Shank Stew

SERVES 8

This stew, like the cinnamon-spice perfume, is reminiscent of Morocco. It is based on veal shank, tomatoes, and onions, to which are added cinnamon, ginger, saffron, and orange zest to create a haunting aroma. A little cayenne is added to cut through the sweetness, and the cinnamon blends so well with the other ingredients that it is hard to discern on its own. For this recipe, I like the soft roundness of the ground cinnamon rather than the penetrating intensity of the essential oil. You can make this the same day, but a day in the refrigerator will improve it. It also freezes well if you have leftovers. If you cannot find shanks, you can substitute any other braising cut of veal.

continued

8 pounds veal shanks, meat cut from the bones into ½-inch squares	12 medium ripe tomatoes (about 5 pounds)
2 teaspoons ground cinnamon	1 teaspoon saffron threads
1½ teaspoons ground ginger	1 teaspoon grated orange zest
⅓ teaspoon ground cayenne pepper	⅔ cup plain whole-milk yogurt
Salt and freshly ground black pepper	¼ teaspoon minced fresh rosemary
1 tablespoon pure olive oil	2 tablespoons chopped fresh mint
4 medium yellow onions (about 2 pounds unpeeled)	

Toss the cubed meat with the cinnamon, ginger, cayenne, and salt and pepper in a large bowl. Let it stand for 20 minutes. Heat the pure olive oil in a large nonreactive pot over medium heat and add the veal, keeping the bowl nearby. Lightly brown the veal for 8 to 10 minutes, stirring often to avoid burning the spices. Transfer the veal back to the bowl. Suspend a basket strainer over the bowl.

While the veal is browning, peel and thinly slice the onions. When you remove the veal from the pan, add the onions and a little salt and cook them slowly, covered, until tender.

While the onions are cooking, bring a large pot filled with water to a boil. Cut a small "x" in the bottom of the tomatoes and blanch them in the boiling water for 10 seconds; remove to a plate to cool. When cool, skin and core the tomatoes, and cut them in half. Squeeze the juice and seeds into the strainer suspended over the veal, and then push the juice through the strainer with a spatula. Remove the strainer, cut the tomatoes into roughly ¾-inch cubes, and put them in the bowl with the veal.

When the onions are tender, add the veal, tomatoes and strained tomato juice, saffron, orange zest, and salt, and cook at a low simmer for 3 hours, or until the veal is tender but not falling apart. Remove from the heat.

Scoop 4 cups of the onions, tomatoes, and cooking liquid into a blender, and blend with the yogurt until smooth. Because the liquid is hot, you should blend in small batches. Return the mixture to the pot with the veal. Add the minced rosemary, stir to combine, and season with salt. If making ahead, cool and refrigerate until needed.

TO SERVE: Reheat the stew if necessary, stir in the mint, and serve immediately. It is great with basmati rice or bread.

Warm Apple-Cinnamon Soup

SERVES 8

This soup is a more sophisticated, grown-up version of hot mulled cider, silky with butter and perked up with Calvados. It is topped with sweet, cinnamon-dusted croutons made from brioche, which add textural contrast. Use sparkling cider for this recipe because it is lighter and less sweet than regular apple juice, and makes for a more elegant soup. The soup can be made a day ahead of time, but make the croutons the same day.

APPLE-CINNAMON SOUP

3 pounds Fuji apples, peeled, cored, and sliced

4 cups sparkling apple cider

6 tablespoons unsalted butter

1/2 cup sugar

2 teaspoons ground cinnamon

1/2 cup Calvados

1 tablespoon plus 1 teaspoon fresh lemon juice

2 drops cinnamon bark essential oil

Salt

CINNAMON-BRIOCHE CROUTONS

3 ounces brioche, cut in 1/2-inch cubes

1 tablespoon unsalted butter, melted

1 tablespoon plus 1 teaspoon sugar

1/2 teaspoon ground cinnamon

Salt

FOR THE SOUP: In a nonreactive pot, bring the apples, apple cider, butter, sugar, and cinnamon to a simmer, and cook until the apples are very tender, about 30 minutes. Puree the mixture and pass it through a basket strainer. Add the Calvados, lemon juice, essential oil, and a pinch of salt. If you are making the soup in advance, cool and refrigerate it.

FOR THE CROUTONS: While the soup is cooking, toss the brioche in the melted butter with 2 teaspoons of the sugar. Bake in a 300°F oven, stirring occasionally, until crisp. Remove the pan and toss the croutons with the remaining 2 teaspoons sugar and a pinch of salt.

TO SERVE: Heat the soup and pour into warm soup bowls. Scatter the croutons on top and serve.

Chocolate-Cinnamon Caramels

MAKES ABOUT 40 CARAMELS

These easy-to-make caramels are wonderfully chewy, and their flavor is a balance of caramelized sugar, cocoa, and cinnamon bark essential oil with no one element completely dominating the others. You can mold and cut the candy into squares, or roll it into truffles. Try adding a little *fleur de sel,* small grains of crunchy sea salt, sprinkled on top just before serving. They will keep for at least one month well covered in the refrigerator—just take them out at least an hour before serving to let them come to room temperature. A carefully wrapped box of these caramels makes a nice holiday present. For this recipe, you will need a candy thermometer (see Sources, page 201).

2 cups sugar

1½ cups heavy cream

2 tablespoons unsweetened cocoa powder, preferably Valrhona

4 drops cinnamon bark essential oil

Salt

Have the cream measured and ready. In a nonreactive pot, preferably one with high sides, heat the sugar over medium-high heat, stirring with a whisk from time to time, until it is a deep brown color. Add the cream carefully (it may splatter), and stir until it is completely incorporated. Put the thermometer into the mixture and continue to cook it until the thermometer reaches 240°F, stirring the mixture constantly. This will take about 10 minutes. Remove from the heat and allow the caramel to cool for 10 minutes, stirring occasionally to help it cool. Stir in the cocoa powder, the essential oil, and a pinch of salt. Pour the caramel onto a sheet pan lined with parchment paper. After it cools, cut it into bite-size pieces. If you are not going to eat the caramels that day, refrigerate them in a sealed container.

BLACK PEPPER~

Black pepper is thought to stimulate the mind and to warm an indifferent heart. Known to the Greeks as far back as the fourth century B.C., it was like gold, a medium of exchange and an article of tribute. Today, it is one of the most important spices for perfumery. The not quite ripe peppercorns are dried, crushed, and steam-distilled to produce an almost transparent oil that becomes more viscous with age, smelling dry, fresh, woody, and warm. Its extreme intensity requires a careful hand in perfuming and cooking alike. A tiny amount is all that is needed to lend a spicy note and an edge to a blend.

Black pepper is a basic elemental seasoning in cooking, so often used that we can forget how exciting it can be. Black pepper essential oil from Madagascar, which is used in the recipes, has an entirely different flavor and aroma—at once spicy, earthy, and floral—from that of freshly ground pepper. Once you start using it, you may become addicted to the way it transforms dishes. When you are using ground black pepper in day-to-day cooking, be sure to grind it as you need it, which will deliver the flavor far more completely.

IN THE EVERYDAY KITCHEN: Use black pepper essential oil to season soups and sauces. It is useful in clear broths, where ground pepper tends to settle to the bottom, and it makes a nice addition to marinades.

BLACK PEPPER, NUTMEG, AND SANDALWOOD BOOKMARK

The dry spiciness of black pepper and the woodiness of sweet nutmeg rest on the sweet and mellow scent of sandalwood, which marries beautifully with the slightly animal aroma of the chamois cloth. In a bookmark or sachet, this scent is congenial and won't intrude or overpower.

10 drops black pepper absolute

20 drops nutmeg absolute

40 drops sandalwood essential oil

4-inch-square piece chamois cloth, washed and air-dried

Mix all of the essences in a small bottle, cap, and shake the bottle to combine them. Leave them to marry for a week. Cut the chamois cloth into strips or whatever shape seems appealing and drop the oil onto the cloth. The scent will fade over time, so keep any excess to refresh the cloth later.

NOTE: Chamois is a soft, treated leather that is used to polish cars and can be purchased in automotive supply stores.

Black Pepper–Scented Pork Shoulder Confit

SERVES 8

This may be the perfect way to cook pork. It has the succulent tenderness of a good steak with unmatched depth of flavor from the long, slow cooking (10 to 14 hours) in its own fat. The combination of the black pepper essential oil and the cooking fat from the pork is magical.

If rendered pork fat is unavailable at your butcher, buy four pounds of fresh pork fat (ask for leaf lard) and render it yourself. To do this, put one cup of water and the pork fat in a large stock pot (the water will help start the rendering process). Cook the fat slowly at first, stirring often, until it has liquefied, at which point you can turn up the heat to medium. Cook it until the fat is clear and light yellow-brown in color, and then strain out any solids and reserve the fat. The pork fat will keep for months in the refrigerator, and it is a wonderful cooking medium for everything from onions to peppers to potatoes, even for sautéing chicken or strongly flavored fish such as salmon or monkfish. If you can't find pork fat, you can substitute pure olive oil.

You may want to make enough pork for leftovers—it is incredibly versatile, and can be used in many ways: diced and heated with tomato sauce for pasta, shredded and heated with barbecue sauce for sandwiches, or served with scrambled eggs for breakfast.

PORK SHOULDER CONFIT

4 pounds boneless pork shoulder

Salt and freshly ground black pepper

1 charred yellow onion (page 32)

1 carrot

$\frac{1}{2}$ bunch fresh thyme

2 to 3 quarts rendered pork fat

$\frac{1}{4}$ teaspoon plus 25 drops black pepper essential oil

CABBAGE SALAD

6 cups thinly sliced red cabbage (about 1 head)

6 cups thinly sliced green cabbage (about 1 head)

$\frac{1}{3}$ cup red wine vinegar

$\frac{1}{3}$ cup fruity olive oil

Salt and freshly ground black pepper

FOR THE CONFIT: Two days before serving the dish, season the pork generously with salt and pepper on all sides, cover, and store in the refrigerator overnight.

The next night around 8 P.M., put the pork in a deep ovenproof pot with lid. Add the vegetables and the thyme to the pot. Heat the rendered pork fat and pour it over the pork, covering it completely. Cook the pork, covered, in a 180°F oven for 10 to 14 hours, so that it will be ready the following morning. (Or you can put it in the oven in the morning and remove it at night.) When the pork is properly cooked, it will be perfectly tender, but not falling apart—it should still have defined texture. Home ovens are often not very accurate at low temperatures, so begin checking it after 8 hours (or sooner if you are curious), and then gauge the remaining time based on how quickly it has cooked to that point.

Remove the pork to a plate, cool, and refrigerate (this will make it easier to cut). Strain, cool, and refrigerate the fat.

Preheat the oven to 250°F. Cut the pork confit into 8 pieces at least $1\frac{1}{2}$ inches thick. Combine 1 cup of the cooking fat, freshly ground black pepper, and the black pepper essential oil in a wide pan over low heat. Add the pieces of pork confit, cover, and place in the oven. After 5 minutes, turn the pork over, then after another 5 minutes, remove the pan from the oven but keep it covered.

FOR THE CABBAGE SALAD: Toss the red and green cabbage with the red wine vinegar and olive oil and season to taste with salt and pepper.

TO SERVE: Making sure that the pork is warm, spoon some of the black pepper–infused fat over each piece, sprinkle with a little salt, and set some of the cabbage salad next to each piece. Serve immediately.

New Harvest Potato Soup

This potato soup is infused with bacon and black pepper, and then poured at the table into bowls containing cooked and diced potato, sour cream, and chives—the traditional baked potato toppings. What really makes the soup special is the black pepper essential oil, with its earthy, dusty, and floral tones.

This dish is best in the early summer, when there are potatoes in the markets that have just been dug, with skins that rub off easily. Some kinds to look for are German Butterball, fingerling, yellow Finn, Ozette, and Huckleberry (purple inside, hence the name). During the winter, Yukon gold can be substituted.

3 pounds peeled and sliced new potatoes	Salt
2 medium yellow onions, peeled and sliced (about 13 ounces unpeeled)	3 quarts water
	¼ teaspoon black pepper essential oil
3 ounces sliced bacon	⅓ cup minced fresh chives
5 tablespoons unsalted butter	1 cup sour cream

Cook ½ pound of the potatoes (2 to 6, depending on size) in well-salted water until tender. Cool and dice into approximately ¼-inch cubes. Reserve.

In a soup pot, cook the onions and bacon in 2 tablespoons of the butter over low heat with salt until the onions are tender. Slice the remaining potatoes and add with the water and some salt; bring to a simmer and cook until the potatoes are very soft. Puree in a blender with the remaining 3 tablespoons butter and the black pepper essential oil, then pass through a soup strainer. Correct the seasoning with salt. Hold warm.

TO SERVE: In the bottom of each of eight soup bowls, put about 2 tablespoons diced cooked potato, then 1½ tablespoons sour cream on top of the potatoes. Finish by sprinkling ¾ teaspoon minced chives over the sour cream, and then place the bowls on the table in front of the guests. Transfer the soup to a pitcher and pour the soup around the potatoes and sour cream.

Grilled Summer Vegetable Salad

SERVES 8

This is a bright salad that makes a perfect hot-weather starter. As it can sit for up to an hour without changing too much, it's great for buffets. It is also especially good served with grilled meat. Though the smoky flavors of the firewood enhance and interact with the aroma of black pepper, you can "grill" your vegetables indoors on a cast-iron skillet.

BLACK PEPPER–LIME VINAIGRETTE
Salt
1/3 cup fresh lime juice
1/3 cup fruity olive oil
14 drops black pepper essential oil
20 turns of a peppermill

6 red peppers
4 yellow zucchini
4 Japanese eggplants
2 red onions
Pure olive oil, for brushing vegetables
Salt and freshly ground black pepper
2 1/2 tablespoons chiffonade of fresh mint

FOR THE VINAIGRETTE: Dissolve some salt in the lime juice, then whisk in the fruity olive oil and black pepper essential oil. Add the freshly ground pepper and adjust the seasoning as necessary.

TO GRILL THE VEGETABLES: Quarter and seed the peppers. Slice the yellow zucchini and the eggplant lengthwise into 3/8-inch strips. Peel and slice the red onion into 1/4-inch slices.

Prepare a fire in a wood or charcoal grill. Alternately, heat a cast-iron skillet over medium-high heat. Brush the vegetables lightly with pure olive oil, then season with salt and pepper. Grill the vegetables until tender, remove to a plate, and let cool. If you are using a cast-iron skillet, this may require adding a little oil from time to time to prevent sticking. Just be sure to use as little as possible so you don't saturate the vegetables with oil. Dice the vegetables into large pieces, roughly 3/4- to 1-inch squares.

TO SERVE: In a mixing bowl, toss the grilled vegetables with the mint, vinaigrette (you may not need all of it), and salt. Adjust the seasonings and serve.

GINGER ~

Ginger essential oil blends well with almost any other essence—spices, woods, citruses, and florals—its sweet and heavy undertones lending warmth and spiciness to a blend. The oil's initial fragrance can be likened to coriander mixed with lemon and orange, but as it evolves, the scent becomes warmer and spicier, eventually fading to slightly citrus and woodsy notes. Although most ginger oil is distilled from the dried stems of this rhizome, the best oils are extracted from fresh ginger.

Ginger is one of the most versatile spices to cook with because it can be used in so many forms, each of which affects aroma and flavor. The juice, spicy, acidic, and intense, is best used in cold preparations, where the volatile oils do not get activated. Grated or minced, ginger provides a powerful kick to both cold and warm dishes; slices give a more subtle flavor and aroma to marinades and infusions. Ginger is congenial with vegetables, meats, and fish, as well as sweet herbs such as basil, cilantro, and tarragon. Look for shiny smooth stems; those that are wrinkled and dull in appearance are old and weaker in flavor and aroma.

IN THE EVERYDAY KITCHEN: Finish stir-frys or noodle salads with a few drops of ginger essential oil. Use ginger oil to spark a citrus vinaigrette or to invigorate gingerbread cookies. The Ginger Vinaigrette (page 161) works well with grilled vegetables, especially eggplant and scallions, and steamed bok choy.

Ginger and juniper combine to create a warming, dry, and invigorating body oil. Bergamot lifts and lends freshness to the blend. Wonderful massaged on tired feet after a strenuous day, it can also be used as a moisturizer that scents the body.

40 drops juniper essential oil

12 drops ginger essential oil

8 drops bergamot essential oil

1 ounce jojoba oil

Add the essential oils to the jojoba oil and stir. Decant into a bottle, screw on the cap, and leave the oils to marry for 2 days.

Oxtail Soup with Carrots, Bok Choy, Ginger, and Soy

SERVES 8

The tail is one of the hardest-working muscles in the cow, and oxtail has an intensity of flavor unmatched by any other cut of meat. Oxtails are fairly gelatinous, needing long, slow cooking to fully develop their distinctive taste and velvety texture. In this dish, ginger energizes and freshens the aroma of the oxtail while merging into the whole as a subtle and refined essence. Its flavor is then reinforced before serving by the addition of a few drops of fresh ginger essential oil. The star anise adds a floral note, and the sweetness of the carrots and baby bok choy balance the dark, salty soy.

Everything can be done ahead of time up until the bok choy is added and the soup is finished, making for an easy but impressive entertaining dish. Serve the soup by itself as a hearty first course, or with rice as a complete meal. If you cannot find oxtails, substitute beef shanks for a reasonable approximation. The soup will keep, refrigerated, for a week.

continued

3 pounds oxtails, cut up (your butcher will do this for you)

Salt and freshly ground black pepper

¼ cup pure olive oil

2 medium yellow onions, peeled and sliced (about 13 ounces unpeeled)

3 medium carrots, peeled and cut crosswise in half

1 cup dry white wine

2 pieces star anise

1 cup peeled and sliced fresh ginger (4 ounces)

10 sprigs fresh thyme

10 cups cold water

½ cup soy sauce

3 heads baby bok choy, cut lengthwise into ½-inch strips

3 drops ginger essential oil

Season the oxtails with salt and pepper, then sear them in a cast-iron skillet or sauté pan in 3 tablespoons of the olive oil until nicely browned.

While you are searing the oxtails, thinly slice 1½ onions. In a large nonreactive pot with a tight-fitting lid, add the remaining tablespoon of olive oil, the sliced onions, and a pinch of salt. Cook, covered, over low heat until translucent and tender.

Preheat oven to 275°F. Add the browned oxtails to the pot, along with the carrots, white wine, star anise, sliced ginger, thyme, water, and soy sauce. Char the remaining ½ onion (see page 32) and add to the pot. Bring to a boil, skimming any foam that rises to the surface as it begins to boil, and then reduce to a bare simmer. Cover, transfer to the oven, and cook for 4 to 5 hours, checking occasionally that the liquid is not evaporating too quickly, until the oxtails are tender. Transfer the oxtails and carrots to a plate to cool. If you want to speed up the cooking process, the oxtails will take only 2 to 3 hours at 325°F. The oxtails can also be cooked at a bare simmer on the stovetop.

When the oxtails are cool enough to handle (but still warm), pick the meat off of the bones (the meat is difficult to remove when cold). Taste the meat and add salt if necessary. Cut the carrots into ½-inch slices. If making the soup in advance, refrigerate the oxtail meat and carrots. Strain the liquid through a fine mesh sieve, discarding the solids. (If you want the broth to be completely clear, pass it through cheesecloth.) Refrigerate the oxtail broth until the fat has formed a solid layer on top. The recipe can be prepared up to this point a day in advance.

To finish the soup, remove and reserve the fat from the top of the broth, which should be slightly gelatinous. Bring the broth to a boil and, if it seems watery or if you want more flavor, reduce it a bit. Add the reserved oxtail and carrot. Taste for seasoning, adding salt if necessary. Add the bok choy and cook until it is tender but retains some texture, about 2 to 3 minutes.

TO SERVE: Ladle the soup into eight warm soup bowls. Heat 3 tablespoons of the reserved oxtail fat and add to it the drops of fresh ginger essential oil. Drizzle 1 teaspoon over each bowl and serve. (The remaining oxtail fat can be saved and used for sweating onions, cooking potatoes, or sautéing a steak, for example.)

Vegetable Salad with Ginger Vinaigrette

SERVES 8

This salad has bright, clean flavors and crisp textures. The ginger is juiced and combined with oil and vinegar, creating a mildly spicy, very fragrant vinaigrette that uplifts the mixture of finely sliced vegetables and cilantro. For the juice, simply grate the unpeeled ginger on the largest opening of a four-sided grater and then use your hands to squeeze the juice through a strainer to remove any ginger pieces.

Use a mandoline to slice the vegetables as finely as possible. This creates more surface area to be coated in vinaigrette, so the salad will be more pungent and flavorful, and it also ensures that each bite will contain a mixture of most or all of the vegetables. This is a perfect salad to precede a rich main course, or to begin a light lunch.

GINGER VINAIGRETTE

Salt

1 tablespoon fresh ginger juice

2 tablespoons champagne vinegar

¼ cup fruity olive oil

4 cups napa cabbage, finely sliced (about ¼ head)

1½ cups finely sliced celery (3 to 5 stalks)

1½ cups finely sliced radish (about 1 bunch)

2 cups finely shaved fennel (1 medium bulb)

1½ cups finely sliced green apple (about 1)

½ bunch fresh cilantro, coarsely chopped (including stems)

Salt and finely ground black pepper

FOR THE VINAIGRETTE: Dissolve a few pinches of salt in the ginger juice and vinegar. Slowly whisk in the olive oil. Taste and add more salt if necessary.

FOR THE SALAD: Combine the remaining ingredients except the salt and pepper in a large mixing bowl. Season with salt and black pepper, then pour three-fourths of the vinaigrette over the vegetables and mix well. Ginger can vary in strength considerably, so you might not need all of the vinaigrette. Adjust seasoning, add more or all of the vinaigrette if needed, and serve.

Prawns and Wild Mushroom Stew with Ginger

SERVES 8

This dish combines prawns, wild mushrooms, and leeks in a buttery ginger-scented sauce. Wild mushrooms to look for are chanterelles, black trumpets, hedgehogs, lobster mushrooms, and cauliflower mushrooms. Use whichever you can find, or you can substitute shiitakes, which have their own distinct personality. Here the ginger is used three ways: minced and sautéed, giving little bursts of flavor; simmered in a stock, lending a sweet perfume; and added at the last minute (as the essential oil), creating explosive fresh ginger aromas just before serving.

1½ pounds mixed wild mushrooms (see headnote)

2½ pounds shelled fresh prawns, shells and tails rinsed and reserved

1 tablespoon pure olive oil

1 ounce dried porcini, wiped clean of dirt

½ cup sliced unpeeled fresh ginger (2 ounces)

3 cups water

2 large leeks, white and light green parts only, rinsed and cut into ½-inch slices

5 tablespoons unsalted butter

Salt and freshly ground black pepper

2 teaspoons peeled minced fresh ginger

2 tablespoons dry white wine

1 teaspoon chopped fresh tarragon

3 drops ginger essential oil

Remove the bottoms and any blemished patches from the wild mushrooms. Reserve the trimmings and cut the mushrooms into bite-size pieces. Rinse them well, drain in a colander, then spread out on a clean towel. You should have about 3 to 4 ounces of mushroom trimmings. (If you are using shiitakes, remove the stems and reserve as trimmings, then cut the caps in halves or quarters, depending on their size. You will not need to rinse them.)

For the mushroom/prawn stock, sear the reserved prawn shells in the olive oil, stirring frequently. When they turn red, add the dried porcini, mushroom trimmings, unpeeled ginger, and water. Bring to a boil, scraping the bottom of the pot to loosen any caramelized pieces. Cook at a moderate simmer for 1 hour, or until the liquid is reduced by at least half and is flavorful. Strain through a fine mesh sieve and reserve.

While the stock is cooking, in a covered pot, cook the leeks gently with 1 tablespoon of the butter and some salt until tender, stirring occasionally. Add a splash of water from time to time if the leeks seem dry. Remove from the heat and hold warm.

To complete the dish, heat 3 tablespoons of the butter in a sauté pan until it starts to bubble. Add the mushrooms and cook over high heat for 1 minute, stirring frequently, then season with salt and pepper and add the minced ginger. Cook for 2 more minutes, or until the mushrooms are cooked and no liquid remains in the pan. Meanwhile, season the prawns with salt and pepper on both sides. Pull the pan with the mushrooms off the heat, add ¾ cup mushroom stock, the wine, cooked leeks, and seasoned prawns; reduce the heat to a bare simmer (the prawns will toughen if they cook too fast). Cook gently, covered, stirring often, until the prawns are just cooked through, pink in color and firm but not hard to the touch. With a slotted spoon, remove the prawns, mushrooms, and leeks, and place them in the center of eight warm soup bowls.

Add the remaining 2 tablespoons of butter to the liquid in the sauté pan and stir over medium heat until the butter is melted and it forms a thin sauce. Adjust the seasonings and add the tarragon and drops of ginger essential oil. Pour the sauce over the prawns and mushrooms. Serve immediately.

CUMIN~

Blending with oil distilled from cumin seeds is difficult, not only because its intensity overpowers almost any other essence, but because its association with certain exotic foods is so strong that it is challenging to come up with a blend that gets someone to smell it afresh. A penetrating, warming, spicy *top note* with a touch of softness, cumin should be used with restraint, though it blends well with coriander, angelica, oakmoss, and lavender.

Cumin is used in two forms in the recipes that follow, the toasted seeds and the essential oil. Cumin works well in an ensemble, such as curry mixtures, but in these recipes it is the defining note in each dish. Cumin has an affinity for summer vegetables and gamy meats, and it can add complexity to vegetables that are simple and sweet, such as carrots.

IN THE EVERYDAY KITCHEN: Cumin essential oil adds a new dimension to black bean soup or a dish of beans and rice. Diluted with pure olive oil, it tastes wonderful mixed with pasta salad or drizzled on a spicy chicken stew.

Here the heavy green quality of the lavender absolute joins forces with the oakmoss, smelling of trees and wet earth, to balance the warm, spicy undertones of the cumin.

5 milliliters (1 teaspoon) jojoba oil (see Note)

4 drops oakmoss absolute

1/8 teaspoon lavender concrete

7 drops lavender absolute

1 drop cumin essential oil

Heaping 1/2 teaspoon grated beeswax

Place the jojoba oil in a small nonmetal container and stir in the oakmoss and the lavender concrete with a stirring stick. Drop in the other two essences. Set aside. Heat the beeswax in a small pan or dish over very low heat on the stove, or on a laboratory hot plate. When the beeswax has melted, add the oils without delay and heat, stirring, for just a few seconds. Pour the mixture into a jar or compact, cover immediately, and let it set undisturbed for 15 minutes.

Cumin Crackers with Eggplant Dip

SERVES 8

This is an easy and fun recipe. The crackers and the dip are wonderful together, and the cumin essential oil makes the crackers aromatic and flavorful. You can make the eggplant dip a day or two ahead of time and keep it refrigerated, but bake the crackers as close to mealtime as possible.

CRACKERS

1 teaspoon cumin seeds

1 cup all-purpose flour

1/4 teaspoon salt

3/4 teaspoon baking powder

3 tablespoons fruity olive oil

9 drops cumin essential oil

3 tablespoons water

EGGPLANT DIP

3 globe eggplants (about 3 pounds)

3 tablespoons fresh lemon juice

1/4 cup fruity olive oil

2 tablespoons chopped fresh cilantro

2 tablespoons minced scallions

1/8 teaspoon cayenne pepper

Salt and freshly ground black pepper

continued

FOR THE CRACKERS: Spread the cumin seeds on a sauté or sheet pan and bake at 325°F, stirring occasionally, until fragrant, about 15 minutes. Cool and grind in a mortar with a pestle (see page 31).

Combine the flour, salt, and baking powder in the bowl of an electric mixer fitted with a paddle attachment. Add the olive oil in a steady stream while mixing at low speed. After the olive oil is incorporated, add the cumin essential oil and some of the water. If the mixture seems to be getting too wet, then do not add the remainder of the water. Wrap the dough in plastic and refrigerate for at least 2 hours, or up to 2 days (past that it will start to oxidize).

When you are ready to bake the crackers, preheat the oven to 325°F. Roll the dough out very thin, to about $\frac{1}{16}$ inch. Cut the dough into whatever shapes you desire, then place the crackers on a sheet pan. Use the tines of a fork to prick the crackers, sprinkle them with a little of the ground cumin and some salt, and bake them until they are crisp and golden brown around the edges, 15 to 20 minutes.

FOR THE EGGPLANT DIP: Preheat oven to 325°F. Prick the eggplants all over with a fork or knife and roast them on a sheet pan until they are tender, about $1\frac{1}{2}$ hours. Cool, cut them in half, and scoop out the insides. Discard the skins.

In a food processor, combine the eggplant pulp with the lemon juice and olive oil and process until mostly smooth—leave a little texture in the finished dip. Add the cilantro, scallions, and cayenne, and season to taste with salt and black pepper.

Cumin-Crusted Lamb Chops

SERVES 8

Cumin pairs wonderfully with lamb. Coating the lamb in cumin and cooking it in olive oil creates a crust where the two elements are distinct yet melded. The sweetness of the accompanying stew of summer vegetables is balanced with chopped niçoise olives. This is a very easy recipe; just be sure to start cooking the stew first and not to cook the lamb over too high a heat or the cumin will burn.

Tomato, Eggplant, and Pepper Stew (recipe follows)

2 tablespoons whole cumin seeds

16 medium lamb chops (or 24 small)

Salt and freshly ground black pepper

2 tablespoons pure olive oil

$\frac{1}{4}$ cup chiffonade of fresh mint

Prepare the vegetables for the stew and begin cooking.

While the stew is cooking, crush the cumin seeds, preferably with a mortar and pestle, until they are a mixture of finely ground and small pieces. Season the lamb chops with salt and black pepper, then sprinkle them generously with the cumin.

When you are about ready to serve the lamb chops and stew, heat the olive oil in a sauté pan over medium-hot heat and sauté the lamb, being careful not to burn the spices. (You can also brown them briefly in the pan and then put them on a sheet pan in a 325°F oven to finish cooking, if you like.) When the lamb is done, remove it to a plate to rest for a few minutes.

TO SERVE: Stir the mint into the stew and divide the stew among eight warm plates. Place the lamb next to the stew and serve immediately.

TOMATO, EGGPLANT, AND PEPPER STEW

1 pound stemmed Japanese eggplants (about 6 eggplants)

1 pound seeded red peppers (about 6 peppers)

1¼ pounds tomatoes (about 6 tomatoes)

2 medium yellow onions, peeled and sliced (about 13 ounces unpeeled)

1 tablespoon pure olive oil

Salt and freshly ground black pepper

3 tablespoons chopped black olives, such as niçoise

Cut the eggplant and red pepper into rough, ¾-inch dice. (Since this is a rustic stew, it's not too important for the vegetables to be the same shape, but they should be about the same size so that they cook evenly.) Cut a small "x" in the bottom of each tomato, and blanch for 10 to 15 seconds in boiling water. Remove to a plate to cool, then peel and core. Cut the tomatoes in half and empty the seeds and juice into a strainer basket set over a bowl. Dice the tomato in the same large dice as the other vegetables and reserve the strained juice. Discard the seeds and skin.

Cook the onions in the olive oil with some salt in a nonreactive pot, covered, over low heat, until tender. Uncover and add the peppers, eggplant, tomato, reserved tomato juice, olives, a little salt, and black pepper, then increase the heat to medium. Cook, covered, stirring occasionally, until the vegetables are tender. Adjust the seasoning and keep warm.

Cumin-Glazed Carrots

SERVES 8

In this side dish, carrots are simmered with carrot juice and tamarind (an Asian fruit) and then seasoned with cumin and lime. The natural sourness of the tamarind and lime balances the sweetness of the carrots. Tamarind paste is sold in individual packages in both Asian and Mexican markets, and often in specialty grocery stores as well. This dish makes a wonderful accompaniment to game, especially duck and squab, as well as lamb.

3 cups Vegetable Stock (page 197)

2 ounces tamarind paste (by weight)

1½ cups fresh carrot juice

6 cups peeled and sliced carrots (about 9 medium-size carrots)

1½ teaspoons whole cumin seeds

Salt

1 tablespoon fresh lime juice

3 tablespoons fruity olive oil

6 drops cumin essential oil

In a nonreactive pot, heat the vegetable stock and tamarind to just below a simmer and let stand, covered, for 15 minutes, stirring often to break down the tamarind. When the tamarind and vegetable stock have combined to form a thick puree, pass them through a basket strainer and return the puree to the pan.

Add the carrot juice, carrots, cumin seeds, and salt and cook, covered, until the carrots are tender.

Remove the carrots, and reduce the liquid almost to a glaze. Add the lime juice, olive oil, and cumin essential oil and return the carrots to the pot, stirring and reducing the liquid until the carrots are evenly covered with the glaze. Adjust the seasonings and serve.

CORIANDER~

The oil distilled from the leaves of the cilantro plant has a suave, floral, herbaceous note. Coriander is uplifting and stimulating, and has the same effect on a perfume blend; it provides life and lift to a heavy composition. Coriander works well with jasmine, frankincense, cinnamon, and bergamot.

Both coriander seed and its essential oil have a fresh, lemony flavor and aroma. Both go well with cumin, as well as basil, mint, and cilantro. A few drops of coriander essential oil can transform fresh tomato sauce, and the ground seeds make a refreshing counterpoint when added to a grated raw carrot salad.

IN THE EVERYDAY KITCHEN: Coriander pairs well with all citrus, especially grapefruit, as well as with cumin, cilantro, and mint. Try adding a few drops to a tomato sauce flavored with niçoise olives and mint, or use equal parts ground coriander and cumin to season most meat or poultry.

CORIANDER AND GRAPEFRUIT BODY OIL

Coriander's leafy green scent has some citrus undertones that are enhanced by the tart sweetness of the pink grapefruit. Together they create a sweet, fresh aroma that lifts your mood. This body moisturizer can also be used as a massage oil.

40 drops coriander essential oil

45 drops pink grapefruit essential oil

30 milliliters jojoba oil

Add the essential oils to the jojoba oil and stir. Decant into a bottle, cap, and leave the oils to marry for a week.

Crab Salad with Coriander Vinaigrette

SERVES 8

This is a cheerful winter dish, with its combination of bright colors, flavors, and textures. Pomelo is a kind of sweet grapefruit available during the winter and early spring, but if you cannot find it, you can substitute pink grapefruit. The aromatic combination of pomelo and coriander in the vinaigrette is surprisingly good. It is best with West Coast Dungeness crab, but it also works well with Maine crab.

CORIANDER VINAIGRETTE

Salt

¼ cup fresh pomelo juice

2 tablespoons pure olive oil

2 tablespoons fruity olive oil

8 drops coriander essential oil

White pepper

Champagne vinegar, to taste

CRAB SALAD

1 pound crab meat, picked over

3 cups thinly sliced spinach leaves

3 avocados, peeled, seeded, and diced

2 cups diced pomelo sections
(1 to 2 pomelos)

2 cups sliced radishes (1 to 2 bunches)

1 cup peeled, cored, and diced apple
(1 to 2 apples)

Salt and freshly ground black pepper

FOR THE CORIANDER VINAIGRETTE: In a mixing bowl, dissolve some salt in the pomelo juice. Whisk in the olive oils and coriander essential oil. Season to taste with salt and white pepper. The ratio of pomelo juice to oil will vary dramatically, depending on the acid-sugar balance of the pomelos. Add more oil or juice, if necessary. If the pomelo juice is very sweet, it may be necessary to add a dash of champagne vinegar.

FOR THE CRAB SALAD: Put all of the ingredients in a large mixing bowl. Dress with the coriander vinaigrette and season with more salt and pepper, if necessary. Divide the salad among eight salad plates or bowls and serve immediately.

Chickpea Dip
with Coriander and Lemon

MAKES 1 QUART

This is an elegant version of hummus, with the flavor of garlic and onions softened from long cooking and perfumed with coriander essential oil. You can brighten the spread even more by stirring in some chopped tomato and cilantro at the last minute. It is even better the day after it is made, when the flavors have had a chance to meld. The chickpea dip can be refrigerated for up to a week, although the aroma and flavor will gradually fade. You will need to soak the chickpeas for twenty-four hours before making the spread.

2 cups dried chickpeas	¼ cup fresh lemon juice
1 medium tomato, roughly chopped	¾ cup fruity olive oil
4 large cloves garlic, peeled	¼ teaspoon cayenne pepper
1 medium yellow onion, roughly chopped	10 drops coriander essential oil
Salt	

Soak the chickpeas in 6 cups of water for at least 24 hours. Make sure that they are not crowded in the container, as they will grow to twice their original size while they soak.

The next day, drain the chickpeas and put them in a pot with 6 cups of fresh water. Add the tomato, garlic, and onion, bring to a simmer, and cook with salt until the chickpeas are very tender, 1½ to 2 hours. Drain the chickpeas through a basket strainer, reserving the cooking liquid. Cool the chickpeas and cooking liquid, and then puree the chickpeas in a food processor with ¼ cup of the cooking liquid, the lemon juice, olive oil, cayenne pepper, and coriander essential oil. Pass the mixture through a basket strainer, season with salt, and refrigerate until needed.

Coriander-Crusted Wild Salmon

SERVES 8

In this dish, wild salmon is dusted with coriander and then sautéed, creating a crust and adding a floral, citruslike note to the fish. The accompanying brussels sprouts are shaved thinly and cooked quickly with shaved fennel over high heat, creating an addictive side dish that may replace your standard brussels sprout preparation at Thanksgiving dinner.

6 tablespoons pure olive oil	Salt and freshly ground black pepper
6 cups brussels sprouts, shaved thin on a mandoline (about 1 pound)	¼ cup cider vinegar
	Eight 5-ounce pieces of salmon
2 fennel bulbs, shaved thin on a mandoline	⅓ cup coarsely ground coriander seed

Heat 4 tablespoons of the olive oil over high heat in a sauté pan large enough to hold the brussels sprouts and fennel. When the oil begins to lightly smoke, add the vegetables. Wait about 20 seconds before stirring so the vegetables will begin to brown a bit on the bottom of the pan—this will give the vegetables a roasted, smoky intensity. Stir the vegetables and add some salt. Continue to cook over high heat, stirring often, until the vegetables are lightly browned and tender. If it seems that the vegetables are cooking too fast, lower the heat to medium. Add the cider vinegar, remove from the heat, and season to taste with salt, pepper, and more vinegar if necessary. The vegetables should have bright acidity to balance the richness of the salmon.

While the vegetables are cooking, season the salmon with salt and black pepper on both sides. Put the coriander on a plate (you will probably not use all of it) and press the presentation side of each piece of salmon firmly into the coriander. Heat the remaining 2 tablespoons olive oil in one or two sauté pans, depending on their size, over medium heat. Place the salmon coriander side down in the sauté pans and cook for about 2 minutes, until the salmon has a golden brown crust. (Do not cook the salmon over too high heat, as the coriander may burn.) Turn the salmon over and cook for an additional 1 to 2 minutes, or until the salmon is translucent in the center but not raw. Drain the salmon coriander side up on a plate lined with paper towels.

While the salmon is cooking, divide the brussels sprout mixture evenly among eight plates, forming a bed of vegetables in the center. Put the salmon on top of each pile of vegetables and serve immediately.

Luxurious

Cognac
Vanilla
Chocolate
Saffron

Threads of saffron. OPPOSITE: Panfried Potatoes with Saffron-Garlic Mayonnaise (page 192).

COGNAC~

Essence of cognac is produced by steam-distilling the lees left by the distillation of grape brandy. It has a sweet, herbal aroma, with outstanding tenacity and great diffusive power. Cognac essential oil works well with bergamot, coriander, lavender, clary sage, and ylang-ylang, lending a fresh, fruity, natural note to the blend.

From a cook's perspective, cognac's rich flavor and aroma work best with other rich or strongly flavored foods, such as foie gras and beef. Cognac and the dishes that call for it tend to be special-occasion dishes, although the Prune-Cognac Sorbet (page 181) is simple and tasty anytime.

Cognac is quite strong in its natural state, so if you want a milder, less alcoholic flavor, you can cook it until it mellows. This usually means reducing the cognac by half its volume. Cognac needs fat or sugar to balance its fiery intensity, and for a simple recipe the next time you make steak, try deglazing your pan with cognac, then adding cream, Dijon mustard, and black pepper, and reducing to sauce consistency.

> **IN THE EVERYDAY KITCHEN:** A splash of cognac does wonders for hot mulled cider, or as a last-minute addition to consommés or poultry gravies. For the flavor without the alcohol, try adding cognac essential oil to finish a cream sauce, or add a drop to mushroom soup.

COGNAC COLOGNE SPRAY

Cognac and tonka bean form the base for this cologne. Tonka is sweet and warm like caramel, the ultimate smooth, powdery note; the slightly winey note of cognac imparts fruitiness and softness. The trio of green herbs—lavender, tarragon, and clary sage—lends freshness to the blend. Wear this spray in the spring, when the air is growing warmer and the days longer.

30 milliliters grape alcohol

20 drops cognac essential oil

12 drops tonka bean absolute

8 drops tarragon absolute

10 drops styrax essential oil

10 drops clary sage essential oil

10 drops lavender absolute

6 drops rose absolute

4 drops ginger essential oil

10 drops bergamot essential oil

5 drops sweet orange essential oil

Pour the grape alcohol into a beaker, measuring cup, or small glass. Drop in the essences, beginning with the cognac, and stir after each addition. Pour into a bottle, cap, and let marry for a week or more. Before using, strain the mixture through a plastic coffee filter fitted with unbleached paper. After filtration, this cologne will be acid green and bright like a peridot. Decant into a spray bottle.

Filet Mignon
with Morels and Cognac

SERVES 8

Although filet mignon is often served with a cognac–green peppercorn sauce, the morels in this recipe make for a delicious variation. Morels are a spring mushroom that tastes and smells like nothing else in the world. Smelling them in their uncooked state, it is impossible to imagine the expressiveness of their flavor and their penetrating aroma once they are cooked. In fact, their flavor is so strong, it may overwhelm the cognac in the finished sauce. If so, add a little more cognac at the end, or a few drops of cognac essential oil, to adjust the balance.

1 leek, white and light green parts only

1¹⁄₂ teaspoons minced garlic

2¹⁄₂ tablespoons unsalted butter

Salt and freshly ground black pepper

6 cups morels, washed and trimmed (see Note)

¹⁄₂ cup Mushroom Stock (page 198)

1 cup cognac

¹⁄₂ cup plus 2 tablespoons Crème Fraîche (page 200)

Eight 5-ounce filets mignons, trimmed

1 tablespoon plure olive oil

Cut the leek in half lengthwise and then crosswise into ¹⁄₄-inch slices. Rinse in cold water and drain. Cook the leek and garlic in 1 tablespoon of the butter with salt, over medium-low heat, in a covered saucepan, until the leeks are tender. Add the morels, mushroom stock, and more salt and simmer, covered, until the morels are cooked through, about 15 minutes. They will be tender but still have texture, and the morel aroma will be very strong. Strain the morels, reserving the liquid and morels separately.

In a nonreactive pan, reduce the cognac by half. (Be careful, as it is flammable and may ignite.) Add ³⁄₄ cup of the reserved morel cooking liquid. Reduce the liquid by a third, and then add the crème fraîche. Cook until the sauce is thick enough to coat the back of a spoon, then whisk in the remaining butter and add the cooked morels; heat until warmed through. Correct the seasoning. Remove from the heat and hold warm.

Season the filets with salt and black pepper and sear in a sauté pan with the olive oil over medium heat until rare to medium rare. Remove to a plate to rest.

TO SERVE: Place a cooked filet mignon on each plate. Garnish with the morels and sauce. Serve immediately.

NOTE: To wash and trim morels, cut the pale stems off, then cut the mushrooms in either halves or quarters, depending on size. Wash them in a bowl filled with water, agitating the mushrooms to remove dirt. Drain them and repeat with fresh water until the water no longer turns dirty. Drain the morels and dry on paper towels. Keep uncovered in the refrigerator for up to 2 days.

Seared Foie Gras with Bacon, Apple, and Cognac

SERVES 4

This unabashedly decadent and totally memorable dish is the only recipe in the book for four people, because, though not that difficult, there is a lot going on at the moment of cooking the foie gras. To sauté eight pieces at once would be a challenge.

Here the quickly cooked foie gras is set on a bed of sautéed onions, bacon, and apple and served with a cider vinegar–cognac sauce. You'll find that the cider vinegar cuts the richness of the foie gras, and the foie gras cooking fat that gets emulsified into the vinegar-cognac sauce gives it a silky texture and reinforces its flavor. The sauce should seem a little unbalanced—too much cognac and too much acidity—in order to balance the dish as a whole.

This is a great dish for New Year's Eve or another special occasion, served with a Cognac Cocktail (page 180) in lieu of the traditional Sauternes.

1¼ cups fresh apple juice

¼ cup cider vinegar

¼ cup julienned bacon

1 cup peeled and thinly sliced yellow onions (1 small onion)

Salt and freshly ground black pepper

1 cup peeled and sliced Granny Smith apple (about 1 apple)

½ cup cognac

Four ¾-inch-thick slices foie gras

¼ cup all-purpose flour (spread out on a plate)

Reduce the apple juice and cider vinegar together until only ¼ cup remains. Hold warm.

While the apple juice is reducing, cook the bacon over medium heat until rendered but still somewhat soft. Remove the bacon to a plate.

continued

Cook the onion in the bacon fat with some salt until tender. Remove to the same plate as the bacon.

In the same pan, cook the apple until tender, then add the onion and bacon. Season the mixture generously with black pepper and hold warm (do this just before cooking the foie gras).

Reduce the cognac by half in a small pot with tall sides (be aware that the cognac may flame up). Add the apple juice reduction and remove from the heat.

Season the foie gras with salt and black pepper and then press each piece lightly into the flour, shaking off any excess. Heat a sauté or cast-iron pan over high heat. Sear the foie gras, shaking the pan after a few seconds so the slices don't stick. The foie gras will start to render its fat and brown. Turn the heat down to medium-high and continue cooking for 1 to 2 minutes per side, then remove the slices to a plate to drain. Reserve the rendered fat. The slices of foie gras are properly cooked when you feel their sides and they are yielding rather than hard (this means the foie gras has warmed all the way through and the hard fat has softened to a custardlike interior). The goal is to have the foie gras well browned on the outside and creamy on the inside. The foie gras will get warm inside, but not hot. If it becomes hot all the way through, it will be overcooked.

Put 2 tablespoons of the rendered foie gras fat in the cognac–apple juice reduction and emulsify the mixture with a handheld immersion blender (see Note). Season with salt, cognac, and cider vinegar as necessary. The sauce should taste strongly of cognac and be very acidic to cut the richness of the foie gras.

TO SERVE: Divide the apple mixture among four warm plates, placing it in the center of each plate. Spoon some sauce around. Place a piece of foie gras on top of the apple mixture and serve immediately with a cognac cocktail, if desired.

COGNAC COCKTAIL
½ ounce cognac

⅓ cup apple juice
¼ cup Champagne

Combine all of the ingredients in a Champagne flute. Makes one cocktail.

NOTE: The type of handheld, battery-operated immersion blender designed (and marketed) to foam milk for coffee is perfect for this recipe. It is inexpensive and can be found at many home and kitchen supply stores.

Prune-Cognac Sorbet

SERVES 8

This is a variation on the classic French dish of prunes and Armagnac. This sorbet communicates the flavors more effectively, and the result is more exciting, with the background notes of orange and spices giving the sorbet an almost gingerbreadlike flavor that yields to a subtle burn from the cognac. Because of the alcohol, the pectin in the prunes, and all the sugar, this will be a very soft, creamy sorbet; make it the day before and freeze it overnight so it has time to set. The best prunes are the ones from Agen in France and it's worth trying to find them, but the success of the recipe does not depend on them. If you are one of those people who are not crazy about prunes, this sorbet may change your mind!

1½ pounds pitted prunes

Grated zest of 1 orange

1½ cups fresh orange juice

4½ cups water

¼ cup sugar

¼ teaspoon ground cinnamon

¼ teaspoon ground star anise

¼ teaspoon ground allspice

¼ teaspoon ground ginger

Salt

1 cup cognac

Bring the prunes, orange zest, orange juice, water, sugar, spices, and a pinch of salt to a boil. Reduce the heat and simmer for 2 minutes. Remove from the heat and stir in the cognac.

Let the mixture cool to room temperature, then puree it in a blender. Pass it through a fine mesh sieve and season to taste with more cognac if necessary, or more salt to sharpen the flavors. Freeze in an ice cream machine according to the manufacturer's directions. Let the sorbet set in the freezer for at least 8 hours before serving.

VANILLA~

The vanilla plant is an orchid, a vine that climbs along tree trunks. Its seedpod exudes one of the most enticing aromas in the vegetable kingdom. The culture and preparation of vanilla involves a kind of alchemy, however. The seedpod has no fragrance when it is gathered, but develops its characteristic scent as it ferments under the sorcery of sun and air during the curing process. As the lower end of the pod begins to turn yellow, it releases a penetrating scent of bitter almonds. By degrees the color darkens, the flesh softens, and the true odor of vanilla begins to develop as the natural fermentation gradually progresses up the pod. The scent of vanilla is universally beloved, and there is no essence that it doesn't combine with beautifully. Vanilla can also be used to enliven bitter blends.

Vanilla is the essence of comfort, familiar to children and adults alike. The flavor is in the tiny seeds, not the pod; these recipes all call for the pod to be split open so the seeds can mingle with the other ingredients, infusing the dish with their sweet aroma. Use only vanilla beans in these recipes, not the extract. The flavors and aromas of the two are like night and day, with the beans delivering the truest, most intense flavors. Tahitian Gold vanilla beans are best, but Bourbon beans are fine as well. Look for beans that are moist and plump. If they are shriveled or dried, chances are that they are old and the flavor will be weak.

IN THE EVERYDAY KITCHEN: After you scrape the seeds out of the vanilla beans, bury the pods in sugar. After a week, the sugar will be perfumed. Use the vanilla sugar to sweeten whipped cream, or in recipes for cookies or cakes. Try using vanilla absolute instead of vanilla extract for a truer flavor (you will need to use less, as the absolute is much more powerful).

VANILLA-LICORICE SOLID PERFUME

The highest concentration of vanilla aroma is in vanilla absolute, a narcotic fragrance that envelopes and seduces with its rich and decadent layers of sweetness. Anise hyssop, sometimes called licorice mint, adds a sweet anise scent. The result is a simple solid perfume that smells like vanilla-licorice candy.

10 drops vanilla absolute

15 drops anise hyssop essential oil

5 millimeters (1 teaspoon) jojoba oil

1/2 heaping teaspoon grated beeswax

Drop the vanilla and anise hyssop into the jojoba oil. Put this bowl aside. Heat the beeswax in a small pan or dish over very low heat on the stove, or on a laboratory hot plate. When the beeswax has melted, add the oils, and heat, stirring, for just a few seconds. Pour the mixture into a jar or compact; close immediately and let it set undisturbed for 15 minutes.

Braised Beef Cheeks
with Vanilla, Saffron, and Orange

SERVES 6 TO 8

Beef cheeks are a dense, tough cut of meat that become incredibly moist and unctuous when braised. The meat is slowly cooked with vanilla, saffron, and orange; tomato and red wine give the cooking liquid acidity and definition. Here the aroma of the vanilla is much more prevalent than the flavor. The intense beef flavor remains the central element in the dish, with the other ingredients contributing a subtle, complex bouquet of aromas and flavors. If you cannot find beef cheeks, substitute short ribs or any other braising cut. You can serve this with the Crushed Yukon Gold Potatoes (page 73), substituting fruity olive oil for the rosemary oil. The beef can be made a few days ahead. Just refrigerate it immersed in the strained cooking liquid, and then reheat it gently in the same liquid.

6 beef cheeks, trimmed of excess fat and sinew (4^{1}/$_{2}$ to 5 pounds)	^{1}/$_{2}$ cup fresh orange juice
Salt and freshly ground black pepper	^{1}/$_{2}$ teaspoon saffron threads
2 tablespoons pure olive oil	1 vanilla bean, split and scraped
2 large yellow onions, peeled and sliced (about 22 ounces unpeeled)	^{1}/$_{4}$ bunch fresh thyme
2 medium ripe tomatoes, cored and chopped	1 cup water
Grated zest of 1 orange	1 cup medium- to full-bodied red wine, such as Merlot or Cabernet

Preheat the oven to 275°F. Season the beef cheeks generously with salt and black pepper. Heat a heavy-bottomed braising pan to high. Add the pure olive oil and sear until the cheeks are browned on all sides. Remove the beef to a plate, turn down the heat to medium-low, and add the onions to the pan along with some salt. Cover and cook until tender, stirring occasionally. The onions will pick up some color from the bottom of the pan, which is fine.

Uncover and add the tomatoes, orange zest, orange juice, saffron, vanilla pod and seeds, and thyme, and stir to combine. Arrange the beef cheeks on top in a single layer, and then add the water and red wine. Bring to a boil, cover, and put in the oven. Cook for 3 to 4 hours, until the cheeks are tender but retain distinct texture. Check this by poking them with a fork, and then if not sure, you can cut off and taste a small piece. Remove the cheeks, strain the liquid through a fine mesh sieve, skim off any fat, and season to taste with salt. Serve the beef cheeks sauced with their cooking liquid.

Vanilla Poached Pears with Sabayon

SERVES 8

In this recipe, the pears are poached in Champagne and vanilla, and then napped with a sabayon made from the poaching liquid, which adds a creamy element and reinforces the vanilla-pear flavors and aromas. The sabayon can be made in a stainless steel mixing bowl, but a well-polished copper bowl will give it added volume and stability.

POACHED PEARS

6 underripe pears, peeled, cored, and halved

3 cups water

2 cups Champagne

2 cups sugar

1½ pieces vanilla bean

2 strips lemon peel

Salt

SABAYON

3 large egg yolks

⅓ cup pear poaching liquid

Salt

1 tablespoon fresh lemon juice

FOR THE POACHED PEARS: In a nonreactive pot, bring all of the ingredients to a bare simmer, cover the surface with a piece of parchment so that the pears do not oxidize, and cook until the pears are tender, about 20 to 30 minutes. Remove the vanilla bean and lemon peel from the poaching liquid, cool the pears and liquid together, and refrigerate if not finishing the dish immediately.

FOR THE SABAYON: Bring a small pot of water to a simmer. Put the yolks, poaching liquid, and a large pinch of salt in a mixing bowl. Place the mixing bowl over the simmering water, and whisk vigorously until it lightens in color, grows in volume, and forms thick ribbons. It will be warm but not hot when done.

TO SERVE: Slice the pears into ½-inch slices lengthwise and rewarm them in ½ cup of the poaching liquid. Divide the pears among eight bowls. Add the lemon juice and pinch of salt to the poaching liquid and spoon 1 tablespoon of liquid over each bowl. Finish the pears with dollops of the warm sabayon.

Vanilla Mousse with Fresh Berries

SERVES 8

This is an all-purpose mousse made by setting a vanilla custard sauce, also called an *anglaise,* with gelatin and then folding in whipped cream. It has a comfortable simplicity that goes best with berries, but is also good with other summer fruits such as peaches or figs. Because both the mousse and berries are soft, they pair well with simple sugar cookies. You can make the mousse the day before.

2 cups milk	⅓ cup sugar
1 vanilla bean, split and scraped	1 sheet gelatin, softened in cold water
7 large egg yolks	½ cup heavy cream

Put the milk in a nonreactive pot. Add both the vanilla seeds and the pod to the milk. Carefully heat the milk, stirring often, until hot but not simmering. Remove from heat.

Make an ice bath by combining ice and water in a large stainless steel mixing bowl and then setting a slightly smaller bowl in the ice water. Set a fine mesh sieve inside of the smaller bowl.

While the milk and vanilla are heating, vigorously whisk together the egg yolks and sugar for 4 to 5 minutes, or until the mixture lightens in color and forms thick ribbons. Stir ½ cup of the warm milk into the eggs, then pour the egg mixture back into the pot with the remaining milk. Cook over low heat, stirring constantly, until the custard is thick enough to coat the back of a spoon, about 5 minutes. Remove the pot from the heat, add the softened gelatin, and stir to dissolve. Pour the mixture through the fine mesh sieve into the bowl set into the ice bath and stir the custard until it is cold.

In a clean bowl, whisk the cream until it forms soft peaks, then fold it into the custard. Pour the entire mixture into a container and refrigerate for at least 3 hours.

TO SERVE: Spoon some of the mousse into bowls and garnish with fresh berries.

CHOCOLATE~

The best chocolate *absolutes* are mouthwatering, without a trace of bitterness or cloying sweetness. Voluptuous, highly nuanced, and comforting, chocolate blends well with saffron, patchouli, amber, jasmine, and, of course, vanilla.

From a cook's perspective, unsweetened cocoa powder is the purest form of chocolate flavor and aroma. Without the cocoa butter to bind it, the cocoa powder is incredibly bitter and intense, with an earthy, expansive aroma that makes it at home in both savory and sweet dishes. Cocoa powder always needs sugar to balance it. The best cocoa powder is made by Valrhona (see Sources, page 201).

IN THE EVERYDAY KITCHEN: Add a few drops of chocolate absolute to chocolate cookies, cakes, or tarts to heighten the flavor and aroma. Omit the lavender from the Lavender Shortbread Cookies (page 89) and replace 2 ounces of flour with 2 ounces of unsweetened cocoa powder to make delightful chocolate cookie or tart dough.

CHOCOLATE AND SAFFRON BODY OIL

Romantic and sensual, this is a body oil that would be appropriate to share with a lover. The earthiness of the saffron marries with the sweetness of the ylang-ylang to bring out the floral complexity of the chocolate note.

10 drops cocoa absolute

5 drops ylang-ylang extra essential oil

2 drops saffron essential oil

30 milliliters jojoba oil

Drop the essences into the jojoba and stir. Decant into a bottle, cap tightly, and leave the oil to marry for 2 days. Shake well before use, as the chocolate needs to be evenly dispersed.

Spiced Hot Chocolate

SERVES 8

This is a delicious way to make hot chocolate. The spices mingle with the earthy chocolate to create an exciting aroma, and the vanilla adds sweetness and depth. You can make this in big batches and keep it refrigerated for up to a week.

1 vanilla bean, split and scraped

6 cups whole milk

2 cups heavy cream

1/4 cup unsweetened cocoa powder, preferably Valrhona

1 1/2 teaspoons ground cinnamon

1 teaspoon ground cardamom

1/2 cup plus 2 tablespoons sugar

Place both the vanilla seeds and the pod in a nonreactive pot, add the milk and cream, and bring to just below a simmer, stirring often. While the milk is heating, mix the cocoa powder, spices, and sugar in a heatproof bowl. Pour the hot liquid over the dry ingredients and whisk to combine. Return the liquid to the pan and cook at low heat, covered, 5 minutes more, stirring occasionally. Strain through a fine mesh sieve, pour into mugs, and serve.

Braised Duck with Cocoa and Mint

SERVES 8

This is a straightforward braised duck dish that gets deep, earthy flavor and aroma from cocoa powder, and a lift from the addition of fresh mint. Crème de cassis, a sweet black-currant liqueur added to Champagne in a kir royale, gives a subtle sweetness. You can substitute chicken, pheasant, or Cornish hen for the duck. Serve with buttered egg noodles, which make a great vehicle for the sauce.

1 tablespoon pure olive oil

8 duck legs

Salt and freshly ground black pepper

2 medium yellow onions, peeled and thinly sliced (about 13 ounces unpeeled)

2 large carrots, peeled and sliced ¼ inch thick

10 sprigs fresh thyme

2 tablespoons all-purpose flour

¼ cup unsweetened cocoa powder, preferably Valrhona

2 cups medium- to full-bodied red wine, such as Merlot or Cabernet

¼ cup crème de cassis

3 cups water

1 tablespoon plus 1 teaspoon chopped fresh mint

1 tablespoon fresh lemon juice

Preheat the oven to 275°F. Heat the olive oil in a heavy-bottomed sauté pan large enough to hold the duck legs. Season the duck legs with salt and pepper and sear over medium-high heat until well browned on both sides. Remove to a plate. Turn the heat down to low and add the onions, carrots, and thyme. Cover and cook until tender, stirring occasionally. Add the flour and cook for 5 minutes more, then add the cocoa powder, red wine, crème de cassis, and water. Return the duck legs to the pot. Place the pan in the oven, cover, and cook until the duck is tender but not falling apart, about 1½ hours.

Remove the duck to a plate and transfer the sauce and vegetables to a small saucepan. Put the duck back in the sauté pan and cover to keep warm while you finish the sauce. Over medium-high heat reduce the sauce by about a third, skimming off any fat or foam that rises to the surface. Add the mint and lemon juice and adjust the seasoning with salt and pepper.

Divide the duck among eight soup plates and ladle a generous amount of sauce and vegetables over each.

Chocolate Financiers

MAKES ABOUT 48

Financiers are small cakes traditionally made of almond meal, egg whites, and brown butter. They have an almost crunchy exterior and a moist, chewy interior, with a nutty, buttery flavor. They are best served while still warm, within about ten minutes of baking. Here the addition of cocoa powder gives them an intense chocolate flavor and aroma, causing the nutty notes to recede into the background.

The best financiers are baked in molds made especially for that purpose (see Sources, page 201), but you can bake them in traditional muffin tins. To do so, fill them only about ¾ inch high for the ideal ratio of crisp/chewy outside crust and moist, dense interior. Because extra batter can be frozen and keeps well for up to two months in the refrigerator, the recipe makes more than you will need for one batch. (You can freeze the financier batter in a tightly sealed container for several months. Defrost the batter in the refrigerator for about twenty-four hours before using it.) For a smaller yield, simply halve the measurements.

9 ounces unsalted butter

11 ounces large egg whites (about 11 eggs)

9 ounces (1¼ cups) sugar

4 ounces (1 cup) finely ground almond meal

2½ ounces (½ cup plus 2 tablespoons) unsweetened cocoa powder, preferably Valrhona, plus more for dusting

2 ounces (scant ½ cup) cake flour

1 ounce (2 tablespoons) honey

1 teaspoon salt

Confectioners' sugar, for dusting

Cook the butter over medium-low heat until it is golden brown and has a rich, nutty aroma. Cool to room temperature and strain through a fine mesh sieve to remove any solids.

In a large mixing bowl, whisk together by hand the egg whites, sugar, and almond meal until just combined. Add the cocoa and cake flour and stir to combine. Add the browned butter, honey, and salt and combine. Let the batter rest in the refrigerator for at least 2 hours.

Preheat the oven to 375°F. Butter and flour the financier molds, then fill them two-thirds full with the batter. Bake for 7 to 9 minutes, until just done. Remove from the oven, let cool 3 to 4 minutes, then remove from the molds (you may need to run a paring knife around the inside to loosen them).

Dust with cocoa powder and confectioners' sugar; serve immediately.

SAFFRON~

The Romans combined saffron with sweet wine and sprayed it liberally around theaters, filling the air with a beautiful and costly fragrance. Saffron absolute has both an intense orange color and a penetrating, honeyed, musky aroma. It transforms florals and other spices in a magical way.

Saffron is a flavor at once elegant and mysterious, and it is as much at home in a rustic preparation such as Saffron-Garlic Mayonnaise (page 193) as it is in a more refined context such as Saffron-Tomato Broth (page 194). Saffron should have an intense aroma when you buy it, fragrant and not at all musty or stale. Buy saffron threads, not powdered saffron. It comes in very small bags, but you will need so little each time that it will last quite a while. Store saffron in the refrigerator.

IN THE EVERYDAY KITCHEN: A pinch of saffron threads will add depth to a fish stew. Onions or fennel mixed with saffron and cooked until tender make an interesting accompaniment to steamed or poached chicken. Use the Saffron-Infused Oil (page 193) to perfume potato puree or soup, or try adding a few drops of saffron absolute instead.

SAFFRON, GINGER, AND BLOOD ORANGE BATH SALTS pictured on page 18

The rich, exotic fragrance of saffron combines beautifully with the voluptuousness of blood orange and its raspberry undertones. Ginger provides the perfect counterbalance with its light, spicy, sharp aroma. The combination is both invigorating and sensual and the salts pick up a lovely orange tinge from the saffron and blood orange.

1 cup fine sea salt	**5 drops saffron absolute**
10 drops ginger essential oil	**10 drops blood orange essential oil**

Place the salt in a bowl, then add the essences drop by drop. Stir the mixture with a stirring stick to evenly mix the oils with the salt. Pour the fragrant salts into a jar or bottle and cover with a tight-fitting lid. Let the salts set for a week, allowing the scents to marry and the salts to absorb them. The finished salts should be enough for two baths.

Panfried Potatoes with Saffron-Garlic Mayonnaise

SERVES 8, pictured on page 174

This is a bold-flavored rustic dish to serve family style or individually plated. The mayonnaise is made like an *aïoli,* a sauce from Provence fragrant with olive oil and garlic. This recipe uses saffron-infused oil instead of olive oil, but you can use a fruity olive oil instead. The saffron oil needs to be made two days in advance. You may want to double the recipe, as once it is strained, it can be kept refrigerated for months. It's a great aroma and flavor component to have handy whenever you want it. Also, if you happen to have rendered duck fat handy, you can use it instead of the olive oil to cook the potatoes in for richer flavor. Accompanied by a salad, this dish makes a nice vegetarian lunch.

SAFFRON-GARLIC MAYONNAISE

1 large clove garlic, peeled

Salt

2 large egg yolks

1 tablespoon plus 1 teaspoon fresh lemon juice

2 pinches of cayenne pepper

1¼ cups Saffron-Infused Oil (recipe follows)

POTATOES

2 pounds potatoes (fingerling, yellow Finn, or creamer (new) Yukon gold), unpeeled

Salt

⅓ cup pure olive oil

FOR THE MAYONNAISE: Cut the garlic clove in half lengthwise, remove the germ (that little piece in the middle—you will need to pry it out of both sides of the clove), and cut the halves into small pieces. Transfer it to a mortar, sprinkle with salt, and grind with a pestle until it forms a pastelike puree (this will take 2 to 3 minutes).

Transfer the garlic to a mixing bowl and combine with the egg yolks, lemon juice, and cayenne. Drizzle in the saffron-infused oil a few drops at a time, whisking until it forms an emulsion, at which time you can increase the flow of oil to a slow, steady stream. When all the oil is mixed in, adjust the seasoning with salt as necessary. The sauce keeps at room temperature for an hour or so, or it can be refrigerated for up to 1 week.

FOR THE POTATOES: Cook the potatoes in well-salted water until tender. Drain and spread them on a plate until they are completely cool. Halve lengthwise.

In a 10- to 12-inch cast-iron skillet (sauté pans are fine as well, but I prefer the slow steady heat of cast iron), heat the olive oil over medium-high heat. Carefully place the potatoes cut side down and cook until golden brown, about 3 minutes. Turn the potatoes and cook 2 minutes more. Transfer to a plate lined with paper towels, sprinkle the potatoes with salt, and serve with the saffron-garlic mayonnaise.

SAFFRON-INFUSED OIL

2 tablespoons saffron threads

2 teaspoons water

2 cups pure olive oil

In a small bowl, combine the saffron and the water. Let the mixture stand for 5 minutes, and then transfer it to a blender. Add the olive oil and blend for 1 minute. Transfer the mixture to a sealed container and store it at room temperature for 2 days, stirring from time to time. Strain through a layer of cheesecloth set into a strainer basket and refrigerate if not needed immediately.

Seared Scallops in Tomato-Saffron Broth

SERVES 8

Seared scallops served in a fragrant saffron and tomato broth makes for an easy yet elegant summer starter. Vary the amount of serrano chile according to the desired level of spiciness; either way, it will not affect the aromatic elements.

Tomato-Saffron Broth (recipe follows)

1½ pounds sea scallops

Salt and freshly ground black pepper

2 tablespoons pure olive oil

Prepare the tomato-saffron broth.

Season the scallops with salt and pepper on both sides. In one or two sauté pans, depending on size, heat the olive oil over high heat. Add the scallops and cook them for about 1 minute per side. (They will continue to cook as you finish plating them, so leave them a bit on the rare side.) Remove to a plate lined with paper towels.

Ladle 3 to 4 ounces of broth into each of eight bowls, depending on how "soupy" you want the dish to be. Divide the scallops evenly among the bowls and serve immediately.

TOMATO-SAFFRON BROTH

1 medium yellow onion, peeled (about 7 ounces unpeeled)

1 teaspoon minced serrano chile

Salt and freshly ground black pepper

1 tablespoon pure olive oil

1 teaspoon saffron threads

2 pounds Roma tomatoes, chopped

3 cups Vegetable Stock (page 197)

½ cup dry white wine

3 tablespoons chopped fresh cilantro

In a nonreactive covered pot, cook the onion, serrano chile, and salt over low heat in the olive oil, until tender. Add the saffron, tomatoes, vegetable stock, white wine, and salt, then simmer until the tomatoes are completely broken down, 20 to 30 minutes.

Pass the sauce through a food mill fitted with a medium screen. Add the cilantro and season with salt and pepper.

Artichoke-Saffron Soup

SERVES 8

In this soup, the floral aromas of artichokes and saffron are combined with spelt, and the soup is given a spicy kick from a highly seasoned onion relish. Spelt, a German grain with a sweet, nutty flavor, is slow to break down, but when it does, as in this soup, it creates a silky, buttery texture. Because there's almost no fat in the soup, the flavors are direct and dynamic.

The garnish for the soup—cooked spelt and spicy onion relish—is put in the bowls and then the soup is poured at the table. Although you can make the soup alone, it really sings with the onion relish. In fact, you may want to double the onion relish recipe, as it is great on sandwiches and meats. Everything in the recipe can be made a day or two in advance and refrigerated until needed.

3 pounds medium artichokes	2 tablespoons tomato puree
3 quarts Vegetable Stock (page 197)	8 sprigs fresh thyme
¼ cup dry white wine	2¼ cups spelt
2 medium yellow onions, peeled and sliced (about 13 ounces unpeeled)	1 teaspoon piment d'Espelette puree (see Note)
1 tablespoon unsalted butter	2 tablespoons fresh lemon juice
Salt and freshly ground black pepper	Spicy Onion Relish (page 196)
2 teaspoons saffron threads	

FOR THE SOUP: Peel the dark green outside leaves off of the artichokes until you see leaves that are half yellow and half light green. With a sharp paring knife, trim the stems by cutting ¼ inch off the bottom; then cut away the dark green outer layer of flesh. Cut away the tough green part of the leaves on the top of the artichoke. Fill a container with the vegetable stock and white wine, and as you finish each artichoke, put it in the container so it doesn't oxidize.

In a soup pot, cook the onions in butter with salt, covered, until tender. Add the saffron, tomato puree, thyme, white wine, vegetable stock, trimmed artichokes, 1¼ cups spelt, and more salt and simmer until the spelt is tender, about 1 hour. Puree the soup in a blender and pass it through a basket strainer.

Thin the soup with water to achieve the desired consistency. Season with the piment d'Espelette, lemon juice, salt, and pepper. If you are not going to serve it immediately, cool and refrigerate. Reheat before serving.

continued

FOR THE SPELT GARNISH: Simmer the remaining 1 cup of spelt in salted water until tender. Drain and reserve a few tablespoons of the cooking liquid (make sure that the liquid is not salty—if it is, add a bit of water to dilute it). You can hold the spelt warm for up to an hour. If you cook the spelt ahead, refrigerate it with the reserved cooking liquid. Reheat both before serving.

TO SERVE: Divide the warm spelt among warm soup bowls (be careful not to get the spelt cooking liquid in the bowls). Put a tablespoon of the spicy onion relish on top of the spelt and set the bowls on the table. Transfer the hot soup to a pitcher and pour it at the table.

SPICY ONION RELISH

1 medium yellow onion, peeled (about 7 ounces unpeeled)

1 tablespoon plus ½ teaspoon pure olive oil

Salt and freshly ground black pepper

1 tablespoon plus 1 teaspoon sherry vinegar

1½ teaspoons chopped capers

2 teaspoons chopped currants

1½ teaspoons chopped fresh oregano

1½ teaspoons chopped fresh cilantro

1½ teaspoons minced fresh cilantro stems

1 teaspoon piment d'Espelette puree (see Note)

Make this relish a day or two ahead or while the soup is cooking. Slice the onion about ¼ inch thick. In a sauté pan over high heat, cook the onion in the olive oil, stirring often; season with salt about halfway through. The onion should brown slightly, but not burn. If the onions start to brown too much, reduce the heat to medium. They should be tender but not mushy. Off the heat, add the sherry vinegar (most of it will evaporate immediately), stir, and remove to a plate to cool. Finely chop the onion mixture and combine it with the remaining ingredients. Season with salt and black pepper.

NOTE: Piment d'Espelette is a kind of pepper from the Basque region of France. It has a spicy, smoky, and sweet flavor (see Sources, page 201). Buy the puree, not the powder.

Pantry Recipes

These simple, core recipes belong in every cook's repertoire. They can all be made ahead, and the stocks freeze particularly well.

Vegetable Stock

MAKES 2 TO 3 QUARTS

This is an incredibly useful and versatile stock. It has a sweet vegetal flavor that can be used in many different ways—as a base for sauces and soups, adding richness and depth without changing the essential flavor of what it is paired with. It keeps in the refrigerator for one week, or you can freeze it indefinitely.

3 medium yellow onions, sliced (about 22 ounces unpeeled)

1 yellow onion, charred (page 32)

4 carrots, peeled and sliced

1 fennel bulb, sliced

2 leeks, white and light green parts only, rinsed and sliced

1 small head celery root, peeled and sliced

½ bunch fresh thyme

4 quarts water

Put all ingredients in a nonreactive stockpot. Bring to a boil and simmer slowly for 2 to 3 hours. Strain through a fine mesh sieve. The stock should taste concentrated and sweet. Cool and refrigerate.

Mushroom Stock

MAKES 2½ TO 3 QUARTS

This is a stock whose flavor is mainly based on shiitake mushrooms. It will vary, however, according to what kinds of mushrooms you are cooking with. Button mushrooms should be avoided, as their flavor is not quite right for the stock. Portobello mushrooms, the big brother of buttons, are fine as long as you scrape out the black gills, which will turn the stock black. It keeps in the refrigerator for one week, or you can freeze it indefinitely.

2 pounds chopped shiitake mushrooms

1 ounce (1 cup plus 1 tablespoon) dried porcini, wiped clean

1 ounce (1 cup plus 1 tablespoon) mixed dried mushrooms (yellow foot, chanterelle, candy cap, etc.)

Scraps from trimming wild mushrooms (or substitute ½ pound portobello mushrooms, black gills removed)

4 quarts water

Put all ingredients in a nonreactive stockpot. Bring to a boil and simmer slowly for 1½ to 2 hours, or until the flavor is good and the liquid has reduced by about a third. Strain through a fine mesh sieve, cool, and refrigerate.

Chicken Stock

Although there are not many recipes in the book that call for chicken stock, this is a good recipe to have on hand. It is quite easy, and if it does not boil, it will be extremely clear and flavorful, perfect for broths and simple soups. Try making a chicken soup with rosemary, or add white beans and greens or vegetables to the broth, and scent it at the end with lavender or thyme. It will keep five days in the refrigerator, or indefinitely in the freezer.

3 pounds chicken bones
(often sold as back and necks)

4 quarts cold water

1 yellow onion, charred (see page 32)

1 carrot, peeled and sliced

1/3 bunch fresh thyme

10 black peppercorns

Rinse the chicken bones, then put them in a nonreactive stock pot and cover them with the cold water. Bring to a boil, and skim any of the foam and fat that rise to the surface. After it has been simmering 30 minutes, add the onion, carrot, thyme, and peppercorns and continue to slowly simmer for another 2 to 3 hours, skimming as needed, until the flavor is clear and the liquid slightly reduced. Strain through a fine mesh sieve, cool quickly, and refrigerate.

Crème Fraîche

MAKES 2½ CUPS

You can buy crème fraîche but, if you choose to make it yourself, the process is quite simple. The time it takes will depend on the buttermilk you use, as some have more active cultures than others, and also on the temperature at which the crème fraîche is held. It seems to work best at 65°F to 75°F, and it can be a little warmer, up to 85°F, but no cooler. Add a little sugar to make a terrific topping for fresh berries; combine it with a pastry cream to make ice cream; use it to add a fresh, tangy note to soups and sauces. Unlike yogurt, it can be boiled when incorporated into a hot dish. It will keep up to two weeks in the refrigerator, but it does not take well to freezing.

2 cups heavy cream

½ cup buttermilk

Combine the cream and buttermilk and leave at room temperature, covered, for 2 to 3 days, until thickened. It will set up more in the refrigerator, so when it is ready, the crème fraîche will have a pleasantly tangy flavor and a texture that is somewhere between softly whipped cream and sour cream.

Simple Syrup

MAKES 2 CUPS

Simple syrup is a mixture of equal parts sugar and water. Often used for sweetening sorbets and other fruit-based desserts, it is good to have around, and it will keep indefinitely at room temperature or refrigerated.

1 cup water

1 cup sugar

In a nonreactive pot, stir the water and the sugar and cook over medium heat, stirring, until the sugar has completely dissolved. Cool and store in a container with a tight-fitting lid.

Sources

FRAGRANCE PRODUCTS AND INFORMATION

For all fragrance products featured in the book, perfumes created by Mandy Aftel, and The Nature Perfume Tutorial and Natural Perfume Wheel.

Aftelier Perfumes
510-841-2111
www.aftelier.com

PERFUME ALCOHOL

Bryant Laboratory
510-526-3141; 800-367-3141
www.bryantlaboratory.com

HYDROSOLS

Aqua Vita
416-405-8855; 866-405-8855
www.acqua-vita.com

Liberty Natural
503-256-1227; 800-289-8427
www.libertynatural.com

GRAPE ALCOHOL

Marian Farms
559-276-6185
www.marianfarmsbiodynamic.com

Vie-Del
559-834-2525
E-mail: info@vie-del.com

ESSENCES

Aftelier Perfumes
510-841-2111
www.aftelier.com

Essential Oil University
812-945-5000
www.essentialoils.org

Sunrose Aromatics
718-794-0391; 888-794-0391
www.sunrosearomatics.com

White Lotus Aromatics
fax: 510-528-9441
www.whitelotusaromatics.com

FOR OILS IN THE UK:

Aroma Trading Limited
New Rookery Farm, Silverstone
Northants, England, NN12 8UP
01 327 858758

Fragrant Earth
Glastonbury
Somerset, England, BA6 9EW
01458 831361
www.fragrant-earth.co.uk

LAB EQUIPMENT

Bryant Laboratory
510-526-3141; 800-367-3141
www.bryantlaboratory.com

SCENT STRIPS

Orlandi
631-756-0110
www.orlandi-usa.com

SKS Bottle & Packaging
518-899-7488
www.sks-bottle.com

Sunburst Bottle
916-929-4500
www.sunburstbottle.com

TOILETRIES SUPPLIES

MangoButter.com
www.mangobutter.com

VINEGARS, CONDIMENTS,
AND DRIED GOODS

Corti Brothers carries an impressive
selection of top-quality products.
It is the only place where you can
purchase the piment d'Espelette, but it
also carries everything from Valrhona
chocolate to dried beans, high-quality
vinegars, spices, and fresh wild
mushrooms in season. They have a
store that you can visit in Sacramento,
California, but they have no Web site.

Corti Brothers
916-736-3800; 800-509-3663

SPECIALTY HERBS

The Chef's Garden grows wonderful
vegetables and herbs on its farm in Ohio,
including many hard-to-find items. Its
prices can be quite high, but the quality
is excellent. Earthy Delights is a company
that sells specialty goods, including
specialty herbs, wild mushrooms, and
other pantry items.

The Chef's Garden
800-289-4644
www.chefs-garden.com

Earthy Delights
517-668-2402; 800-367-4709
www.earthy.com

WILD MUSHROOMS AND TRUFFLES

Connie Green, the owner of Wine Forest,
is one of the foremost experts on wild
mushrooms in the country, and her mushrooms are of the highest quality. She also
sells excellent truffle oil, both white and
black, and fresh truffles in season.

Wine Forest Wild Mushrooms
707-944-8604
www.wineforest.com

OLIVE OIL

One of the oldest producers of olive oil
in California, the Sciabica family makes
the most consistently high-quality oils
in the country, and their prices are
reasonable. Their Mission Trail oil is a
good pure olive oil, and Marsala is
recommended as the fruity olive oil
called for in many of the recipes.

Sciabica's
209-577-5067; 800-551-9612
www.sciabica.com

As the name implies, the Rare Wine Company is primarily an importer of fine and rare wines, but it also imports some of the best green olive oils from Tuscany, as well as a wonderful selection of *tradizionale* balsamic vinegar.

The Rare Wine Company
707-996-4484; 800-999-4342
www.rarewineco.com

Tribute Tea is a San Francisco company founded by two doctors. It sells very high quality teas and tea accessories.

Tribute Tea
415-641-8381
www.tributetea.com

J. B. Prince is a New York–based company that sells anything you will ever want or need for your kitchen, from knives to molds, baking supplies, and other equipment. It is quite reliable.

J. B. Prince
212-683-3553; 800-473-0577
www.jbprince.com

Acknowledgments

I would like to thank a few people for their help and support. Eleanor Bertino for bringing me together with Daniel; the team at Artisan, especially Vivian Ghazarian for coming up with such a beautiful design and Amy Corley for her belief in the book and her commitment to getting the word out. my agent, Amy Williams, for her enthusiasm and generous spirit. Jody Hansen, for her graphic genius and patience with my artisan nature; Kaysi Contreras, my assistant, for diving in and doint it; Chris Chapman for designing and creating a perfume studio that exceeded wildest dreams; and Becky Saletan for being my best friend and enriching my life in every possible way.

—M. A.

I would like to thank Eleanor Bertino for connecting me with Mandy, and Mandy for introducing me to the magical world of essences. Thank you to everyone at Artisan for taking a chance on something new, and for shaping our rough ideas into a book: Vivian Ghazarian for the wonderful design; Nancy Murray for supervising production; and Amy Corley for her enthusiastic publicity support and expertise. A warm thank you to my agent, Sarah Jane Freymann, who has helped me in so many ways. Thank you to Peter Thiel and Andrew McCormack for their vision, intelligence, and above all, their trust in my abilities. To my friends who read drafts, tasted and critiqued dishes, and offered support in myriad forms, thank you: Joel Muchmore and Debbie Glass; the Weber family; Soyoung and Jamie Scanlan; Harold McGee; Sean Thackrey, Myron and Liz Udo, Joel Peterson, Mady Denninger, and the Chalk family; David Kinch; Paula Wolfert and Bill Bayer; Laura Chenel and John Van Dyke; Paul Costigan; Dino Copses; Rob Curtin, John Coon, and families; John O'Neill and Randy Hurtado; and Peter Birmingham. I would like to thank my family, especially my father, for his consistent support over many years, and Nana and Papa, who taught me about generosity of spirit and that cooking can be a way of expressing love. Finally, I owe a tremendous debt of gratitude to my cooks. I would especially like to thank Garrett Melkonian for the lemon verbena lemonade idea; Jackie Riley for her insightful flavor combinations and incredible palate; Ron Boyd, for his creativity, passion, and many recipe ideas; and most of all, Phil Ogeila for helping me with a few base recipes, teaching me about baking, and inspiring me with his drive for perfection.

—D.P.

Index

A

absolutes, 20

almond and chamomile soufflé cake, 104

appetizers:

  chickpea dip with coriander and lemon,
    171

  cumin crackers with eggplant dip,
    165–66

  cumin-glazed carrots, 168

  glazed porcini, 130

  morels and spring vegetables with black
    truffle oil, 137

  panfried potatoes with saffron-garlic
    mayonnaise, 192–93

  porcini tart with walnuts and wild arugula,
    132–33

  prawns and wild mushroom stew with
    ginger, 162–63

  seared foie gras with bacon, apple, and
    cognac, 179–80

  seared scallops in tomato-saffron broth,
    194

  steamed artichokes with litsea cubeba
    mayonnaise, 95

  tuna-tomato tartare with lime vinaigrette,
    51

  yellow corn pudding glazed with white
    truffle butter, 138–39

  yellowtail tartare with shiso, 83

apple:

  -cinnamon soup, warm, 151

  in crab salad with coriander vinaigrette,
    170–71

  seared foie gras with bacon, cognac,
    and, 179–80

  in vegetable salad with ginger vinaigrette,
    161

aroma, emotional associations of, 11

artichoke(s):

  -saffron soup, 195–96

  steamed, with litsea cubeba mayonnaise, 95

asparagus:

  in seared scallops with tarragon sabayon,
    77–78

  soup, mint-infused, 39

avocado:

  blood orange and fennel salad with, 55–56

  in crab salad with coriander vinaigrette,
    170–71

B

bacon:

  in new harvest potato soup, 156

  seared foie gras with apple, cognac, and,
    179–80

  in sweet onion–rosemary soup, 70

balsams, 20

basil:

  flageolet, and tomato salad, 58

  mint, and coriander bath salts, 39

bass:

  black, with litsea cubeba and saffron-citrus
    sauce, 96–97

  sea, with rosewater beurre blanc and
    porcini, 116–17

bath oils:

  lime and fir, 50

  litsea cubeba and cedarwood, 95

  tarragon, 76

bath salts, 22

  mint, basil, and coriander, 39

  saffron, ginger, and blood orange, 192

  sweet orange, ylang-ylang, and geranium,
    55

beef:

  cheeks, braised, with vanilla, saffron, and
    orange, 184

  filet mignon with morels and cognac, 178–79

  grilled steak with onion-potato compote
    scented with lavender, 87

greens (continued)

romaine, in jasmine-steamed chicken breast, 112–13

wild arugula, porcini tart with walnuts and, 132–33

green tea, 140

and orange solid perfume, 141

panna cotta, 144

—pistachio crusted cod, 141–42

—scented chicken soup, 143

H

halibut, steamed:

with lemon-chamomile sauce, 102–3

wrapped in napa cabbage with mint, 41–42

haricots verts, for veal tenderloin slow cooked in lemon verbena butter, 62–63

herbal aromas, 68–89

see also lavender; perilla; rosemary; tarragon

honey-lemon glazed turnips, for green tea–pistachio crusted cod, 141–42

hydrosols, 20

I

ice cream, coffee-date, with candied orange, 128

ingredient basics, 28–30

J

jam, plum jasmine, 113

jasmine, 110

liquid perfume, 111

-plum jam, 113

-steamed chicken breast, 112–13

—white peach sorbet, 111

juniper and ginger body oil, 159

K

kitchen tools, 30–31

L

lamb:

chops, cumin-crusted, 166–67

loin poached in rosemary oil with crushed potatoes, 73–74

lavender, 85

cologne spray, 86

cumin and oakmoss solid perfume with, 165

grilled steak with onion-potato compote scented with, 87

—lemon verbena mist, 60

roasted chicken, 88

shortbread cookies, 89

leeks:

for chamomile-scented veal tenderloin, 100–101

in green tea–scented chicken soup, 143

in monkfish roasted on a bed of rosemary, 71–72

in winter vegetable curry accented with orange flower water, 106–7

lemon:

-chamomile sauce, steamed halibut with, 102–3

chickpea dip with coriander and, 171

-honey glazed turnips, for green tea–pistachio crusted cod, 141–42

lemongrass:

in lemon verbena butter, veal tenderloin slow cooked in, 62–63

-porcini consommé, 131

lemon verbena, 59

butter, veal tenderloin slow cooked in, 62–63

—lavender mist, 60

"lemonade," 60

-strawberry granita, 61

natural essences (continued)

    safe use of, 17

    storage of, 26

    useful tools for, 22–23

    workspace for, 25

neroli, 105

    rose and frankincense face elixir with, 115

    see also orange flower

nutmeg, black pepper, and sandalwood
    bookmark, 154

O

oakmoss, cumin, and lavender solid perfume,
    165

odors, unwanted, 34

oils, essential, *see* essential oils

oils, vegetable, 30

olfactory fatigue, 26

olive vinaigrette, 74

onion(s):

    charring, 32

    -lime sauce, for duck legs braised with red
        wine and lime, 52–53

    in morels and spring vegetables with
        black truffle oil, 137

    in Moroccan veal shank stew, 149–50

    pearl, in poached chicken with tarragon,
        79

    -potato compote scented with lavender,
        grilled steak with, 87

    relish, spicy, for artichoke-saffron soup,
        195–96

    in seared foie gras with bacon, apple, and
        cognac, 179–80

    sweet, and rosemary soup, 70

    in turnip soup with perilla-infused oil, 82

orange, 54

    bitter orange vinaigrette, for flageolet,
        tomato, and basil salad, 58

    braised beef cheeks with vanilla, saffron,
        and, 184

    candied, coffee-date ice cream with, 128

    and green tea solid perfume, 141

    -mint compote, spicy, pork loin paillards
        with, 56–57

    ylang-ylang and geranium bath salts with,
        55

orange, blood:

    fennel and avocado salad with, 55–56

    saffron and ginger bath salts, 192

    and white truffle solid perfume, 135

orange flower, 105

    custard, 109

    and sandalwood mist, 106

    water, dried fruits marinated in, 108–9

    winter vegetables curry accented with,
        106–7

P

paillards, pork loin, with spicy orange-mint
    compote, 56–57

panna cotta, green tea, 144

parfum de Maroc, 149

parsnip-potato puree, for pork chop with
    coffee-fig sauce, 126–27

pears, vanilla poached, with sabayon, 185

peas, green:

    in jasmine-steamed chicken breast,
        112–13

    in morels and spring vegetables with
        black truffle oil, 137

    in seared scallops with tarragon sabayon,
        77–78

peppers:

    in grilled summer vegetable salad, 157

    tomato and eggplant stew with, for
        cumin-crusted lamb chops,
        166–67

perfumer's pantry, 19–26

    concretes and absolutes in, 20

    essential oils in, 19–20

    fragrances and carriers in, 21–22

    hydrosols in, 20

    and making fragrance, 24–25

resins and balsams in, 20

sources of, 201–3

useful tools in, 22–23

see also natural essences

perilla (shiso), 80

in heirloom tomato and Yellow Doll
watermelon salad, 84

-infused oil, turnip soup with, 82

and rose bookmark, 81

yellowtail tartare with, 83

pineapple–litsea cubeba granita, 98

pistachio–green tea crusted cod,
141–42

plum-jasmine jam 113

pomelo, in crab salad with coriander
vinaigrette, 170–71

porcini, *see* cèpe

pork:

chop with coffee-fig sauce, 126–27

loin paillards with spicy orange-mint
compote, 56–57

shoulder confit, black pepper–scented,
154–55

potato(es):

crushed, lamb loin poached in rosemary
oil with, 73–74

-onion compote scented with lavender,
grilled steak with, 87

panfried, with saffron-garlic mayonnaise,
192–93

-parsnip puree, for pork chop with coffee-
fig sauce, 126–27

in poached chicken with tarragon, 79

soup, new harvest, 156

prawns and wild mushroom stew with ginger,
162–63

product sources, 201–3

prune-cognac sorbet, 181

Q

quinoa, for steamed halibut wrapped in napa
cabbage with mint, 41–42

R

radicchio, for pork loin paillards with spicy
orange-mint compote, 56–57

radish(es):

in crab salad with coriander vinaigrette,
170–71

cucumber, and fennel salad, for chilled
cucumber consommé, 45–46

endive and apple salad with, for mint-
infused asparagus soup, 39–40

tarragon-marinated beets with frisée and,
76–77

in vegetable salad with ginger vinaigrette,
161

ras el hanout, 149

red wine:

in braised beef cheeks with vanilla, saffron,
and orange, 184

in braised duck with cocoa and mint, 189

duck legs braised with lime and, 52–53

refreshing aromas, 38–63

see also cucumber; lemon verbena; lime;
orange; spearmint

relish, spicy onion, for artichoke-saffron soup,
195–96

resins, 20

romaine:

for black bass with litsea cubeba and
saffron-citrus sauce, 96–97

in jasmine-steamed chicken breast, 112–13

rose, 114

and ginger soufflé, 118

neroli, and frankincense face elixir, 115

and perilla bookmark, 81

rosemary, 68

cologne spray, 69

and cucumber mist, 45

-infused oil, for sweet onion–rosemary
soup, 70

monkfish roasted on a bed of, 71–72

oil, lamb loin poached in, with crushed
potatoes, 73–74

–sweet onion soup, 70

green tea–scented chicken, 143

mint-infused asparagus, 39–40

new harvest potato, 156

oxtail, with carrots, bok choy, ginger, and
soy, 159–61

porcini-lemongrass consommé, 131

sweet onion–rosemary, 70

turnip, with perilla-infused oil, 82

warm apple-cinnamon, 151

see also stocks

spearmint, 38

spelt garnish, for artichoke-saffron soup,
195–96

spicy aromas, 148–72

see also black pepper; cinnamon;
coriander; cumin; ginger

spinach:

baby, for monkish roasted on bed of
rosemary, 71–72

in crab salad with coriander vinaigrette,
170–71

stews:

Moroccan veal shank, 149–50

prawns and wild mushroom, with ginger,
162–63

tomato, eggplant, and pepper, for cumin-
crusted lamb chops, 166–67

winter vegetable curry accented with
orange flower water, 106–7

stocks:

chamomile, for chamomile-scented veal
tenderloin, 100–101

chicken, 199

corn, for yellow corn pudding glazed with
white truffle butter, 138–39

mushroom, 198

vegetable, 197

straining soups and sauces, 33

strawberry:

marinated in rosewater, 115

-verbena granita, 61

syrups:

jasmine, in white peach–jasmine sorbet,
111

lemon verbena, in "lemonade," 60

simple, 200

T

tapioca, for dried fruits marinated in orange
flower water, 108–9

tarragon, 75

bath oil, 76

-marinated beets with frisée and radishes,
76–77

poached chicken with, 79

sabayon, seared scallops with, 77–78

tartare:

tuna-tomato, with lime vinaigrette, 51

yellowtail, with shiso, 83

tomato(es):

eggplant and pepper stew with, for
cumin-crusted lamb chops, 166–67

flageolet and basil salad with, 58

heirloom, and Yellow Doll watermelon
salad, 84

in Moroccan veal shank stew, 149–50

-saffron broth, seared scallops in, 194

-tuna tartare with lime vinaigrette, 51

truffle, 134

truffle, black:

—balsamic vinaigrette, mixed chicory
salad with, 136

oil, morels and spring vegetables with,
137

truffle, white:

and blood orange solid perfume, 135

butter, yellow corn pudding glazed with,
138–39

truffles, chocolate-mint, 43

tuberose and cèpe perfume, 130

tuna-tomato tartare with lime vinaigrette,
51

turnips:

honey-lemon glazed, for green tea–
pistachio crusted cod, 141–42

soup with perilla-infused oil, 82